ENDGA~~

The Ashbin Play

TWAYNE'S MASTERWORK STUDIES

Robert Lecker, General Editor

ENDGAME

The Ashbin Play

Arthur N. Athanason

TWAYNE PUBLISHERS • NEW YORK
Maxwell Macmillan Canada • Toronto
Maxwell Macmillan International • New York   Oxford   Singapore   Sydney

Twayne's Masterwork Studies No. 109

Endgame: The Ashbin Play
Arthur N. Athanason

Twayne Publishers
Macmillan Publishing Company
866 Third Avenue
New York, New York 10022

Maxwell Macmillan Canada, Inc.
1200 Eglinton Avenue East
Suite 200
Don Mills, Ontario M3C 3N1

Library of Congress Cataloging-in-Publication Data
Athanason, Arthur N.
   Endgame: the ashbin play / Arthur N. Athanason.
     p.   cm. — (Twayne's masterwork studies; no. 109)
   Includes bibliographical references and index.
   ISBN 0-8057-9416-6. — ISBN 0-8057-8576-0 (pbk.)
   1. Beckett, Samuel, 1906–1989 Fin de partie.
   I. Title. II. Series.
PQ2603.E378F5817 1993
843'.912—dc20
                                    92-47351
                                        CIP

The paper used in this publication meets the minimum requirements of American National Standard for Information Sciences—Permanence of Paper for Printed Library Materials. ANSI Z3948-1984. ∞™

10 9 8 7 6 5 4 3 2 1 (hc)
10 9 8 7 6 5 4 3 2 1 (pb)

Printed in the United States of America

To my father, Colonel Nicholas A. Athanason,
and to my devoted friend, Mary Davis,
for sharing my journey

VERDOUX: It's the approach of death that terrifies.

GIRL (*Meditatively*): I suppose if the unborn knew of the approach of life, they'd be just as terrified.
    —*Monsieur Verdoux* (1947), screenplay by Charles Chaplin

Contents

Samuel Beckett in the mid-1980s
© *Jerry Bauer*

Note on the References and Acknowledgments

This study, as well as the series in which it appears, is addressed to the general reader in the home, library, or classroom who wishes to engage with one of the major works in world literature so as to appreciate its riches and wonders. My specific intention, however, has been to approach Samuel Beckett's remarkable one-act play as an 85-minute piece of compelling theater rather than as a biblical or philosophical "mind game" already well documented by others—and to let Beckett, his four shelter-bound characters, and his major critics speak for themselves whenever possible.

Quotations from *Endgame* throughout this study refer to the Grove Press paperback edition (which also includes *Act without Words: A Mime for One Player*), first published in 1958, and are reprinted by permission of Grove Weidenfeld, a division of Grove Press, Inc. Copyright © 1958 by Grove Press, Inc.; copyright renewed © 1986 by Samuel Beckett. The strikingly appropriate "ashbin" photoportrait of Beckett has been reproduced here by special permission of its photographer, Jerry Bauer.

I also wish to express my appreciation to my colleague and friend Clinton S. Burhans, Jr., for his invaluable advice and practical suggestions throughout the research and writing of this study, and my heartfelt gratitude, as always, to my dear and devoted friend Mary F. S. Davis, for reading the working drafts of the manuscript, chapter by chapter, with her customary scrupulous rigor.

Chronology:
Samuel Beckett's Life and Works

1906   Good Friday, 13 April, Samuel Barclay Beckett born at Foxrock, near Dublin, second son of William Frank Beckett, Jr., and Mary Jones Roe Beckett, prosperous middle-class Anglo-Irish Protestant descendants of seventeenth-century French Huguenots who fled to Ireland to avoid religious persecution. Father, William (Bill) Beckett, is quantity surveyor (building contractor), with more regard for sports than intellectual or aesthetic endeavor. Mother, Mary (May) Beckett, strong-willed and independent, trained as nurse in Dublin hospital before marriage. First son, Frank Edward Beckett (born 26 July 1902), eventually becomes manager and heir to father's quantity surveying firm.

1911–1923   After attending Miss Ida Elsner's Academy in Stillorgan, sent to Earlsfort House School in Dublin (1911–19), then in 1919, to Portora Royal School in Enniskillen, Northern Ireland.

1923–1927   Pensioner at Trinity College, Dublin, then foundation scholar, studying French and Italian; graduates first in class, 1927.

1928   Spends spring term as French tutor at Campbell College, Belfast; in October, departs for Paris to begin two-year exchange lecturership at l'École Normale Supérieure; meets James Joyce and other writers associated with *transition*, influential review magazine.

1929   Begins literary career. First fiction ("Assumption" and "Che Sciagura") published, and first criticism ("Dante . . . Bruno. Vico . . . Joyce") included in collection of essays in response to critics of Joyce's *Work in Progress*.

Chronology

1930   Wins first-place prize from Hours Press for poem on Descarte ("Whoroscope"); returns to Dublin to begin three-year lectur-ership in French at Trinity College.

1931   For Trinity's annual drama festival, coauthors (with George Pelorson) and acts in his first play, *Le Kid,* parody of Corneille's *Le Cid; Proust* monograph published; receives M.A. from Trinity, and resigns lecturership.

1932   After period of restless foreign travel, returns to Dublin; starts novel, *Dream of Fair to Middling Women.*

1933   Abandons *Dream . . .* as novel, using some of its material in collection of short stories, *More Pricks than Kicks;* his father dies in June; £200 yearly annuity, administered by his mother, becomes bulk of his income until royalties from *Waiting for Godot* 20 years later; moves to London to pursue journalism.

1934   *More Pricks than Kicks* published; starts *Murphy.* Begins psy-choanalysis with Dr. Wilfred Brion at the Tavistock Clinic.

1935   *Echo's Bones and Other Precipitates* (first collection of poems) published.

1936   Finishes *Murphy,* first completed novel.

1937   Begins and abandons play entitled *Human Wishes,* speculating on nature of relationship between Dr. Samuel Johnson and Mrs. Hester Thrale, widow who after four years' dalliance married another man. Moves permanently to Paris, returning to Dublin thereafter for visits only.

1938   *Murphy* published by Routledge, after rejection by 42 other publishers. On 7 January, stabbed on Paris street; while in hos-pital, visited by pianist Suzanne Deschevaux-Dumesnil, who, in 1961, becomes his wife.

1942   Resistance group in which Beckett has been active for two years betrayed to the gestapo; escapes with Suzanne Deschevaux-Dumesnil to Roussillon in unoccupied southern France, where they remain until end of war.

1942–1945   Works as farm laborer near Avignon; writes *Watt,* his last English novel.

1945   Receives *Croix de Guerre* and *Médaille de la Résistance;* accepts post as interpreter and storekeeper at Irish Red Cross Hospital, Saint-Lô, Normandy.

1946–1950   Returns to Paris and begins most productive period, writing regularly in French: 1946, *Mercier et Camier* and *Nouvelles;*

1947, *Éleuthéria* (unpublished) and *Molloy;* 1948, *Malone meurt (Malone Dies);* 1949, *En attendant Godot* and *Three Dialogues;* 1950, *L'Innommable (The Unnamable).* His mother dies in August. Trilogy, *Molloy, Malone meurt,* and *L'Innommable,* accepted for French publication by Editions de Minuit.

1952   *En attendant Godot* published in Paris.

1953   World premiere, 5 January, of *En attendant Godot,* at Théâtre de Babylone, Paris, directed by Roger Blin; *Watt* published in Paris.

1954   *Waiting for Godot* published in New York; Beckett's only brother, Frank, dies.

1955   World premiere, 3 August, of *Waiting for Godot* at Arts Theatre Club, London, directed by Peter Hall. *Nouvelles et Textes pour rien (Stories and Texts for Nothing)* published in Paris.

1956   First American production of *Waiting for Godot* at Coconut Grove Playhouse, Coral Gables, Florida, directed by Alan Schneider; subsequently opens in New York, directed by Herbert Berghof. *Fin de partie (Endgame)* completed.

1957   *All That Fall* broadcast 13 January, on BBC Third Program, directed by Donald McWhinnie; world premiere, 3 April, of *Fin de partie (Endgame)* and *Acte sans paroles I (Act without Words I)* at Royal Court Theatre, London, directed by Roger Blin.

1958   First English production of *Endgame,* at Cherry Lane Theatre, New York, directed by Alan Schneider; world premiere, 28 October, of *Krapp's Last Tape,* at Royal Court Theatre, London, directed by Donald McWhinnie.

1959   *Embers* broadcast 24 June, on BBC Third Program. Beckett receives honorary degree from Trinity College, Dublin. *Embers* wins Italia Prize.

1961   *Comment c'est (How It Is)* published in Paris; *Poems in English* published in London; world premiere, 17 September, of *Happy Days* at Cherry Lane Theatre, New York, directed by Alan Schneider. With Jorge Luis Borges, Beckett shares the International Publishers' Prize.

1962   *Words and Music* broadcast 13 November, on BBC Third Program.

1963   World premiere, 16 June, of *Play,* in German, at Ulm-Donau, directed by Deryk Mendel; *Cascando* broadcast in French 13 October, on ORTF, directed by Roger Blin.

Chronology

1964	*Play* first performed in English, at Cherry Lane Theatre, New York. In July, travels to New York to assist with filming of *Film* (starring Buster Keaton), directed by Alan Schneider. *Cascando* broadcast in English 6 October, on BBC Third Program.
1965	*Come and Go,* in German, performed at Schiller-Theater Werkstatt, Berlin, directed by Deryk Mendel. *Imagination Dead Imagine* published in London.
1966	Directs first production of *Va et vient* (*Come and Go*) in Paris, then German television version of *Eh Joe; Eh Joe* broadcast 4 July, on BBC Television, directed by Alan Gibson and Beckett.
1967	Directs *Endgame* in German (*Endspiel*), 25 September, at Schiller-Theater Werkstatt, Berlin.
1969	Awarded Nobel Prize in literature, 23 October, but declines to travel to Stockholm for presentation. *Breath* (originally incorporated by Kenneth Tynan as opening sketch in *Oh! Calcutta!*) performed by itself for first time in Glasgow, directed by Geoffrey Gilham. Directs *Krapp's Last Tape* in German at Schiller-Theater Werkstatt, Berlin.
1970	Directs *Krapp's Last Tape* in French and *Act without Words I and II* at Petit d'Orsay, Paris.
1971	Directs *Happy Days* in German at Schiller-Theater Werkstatt for Berlin Festival.
1972	*The Lost Ones* published in New York; world premiere, 22 November, of *Not I,* in Lincoln Center Forum, New York: Jessica Tandy as Mouth and Henderson Forsythe as Auditor; Alan Schneider, director.
1975	Directs *Waiting for Godot* in German at Schiller-Theater Werkstatt, Berlin, and *Not I* in French at Petit d'Orsay, Paris.
1976	Directs *That Time* and *Footfalls* premiere for his seventieth birthday celebration at Royal Court Theatre, London; *Radio II* (*Rough for Radio*) broadcast 13 April, on BBC Third Program.
1977	*Ghost Trio* and . . . *but the clouds* . . . broadcast 17 April, on BBC Television, with Billie Whitelaw and Ronald Pickup, directed by Donald McWhinnie.
1978	*Poèmes suivi de mirlitonnades,* 35 short poems in French written 1976–78, published in Paris.
1979	Directs *Happy Days* (starring Billie Whitelaw) in London.
1980	World premiere, 14 December, of *A Piece of Monologue,* performed by David Warrilow at La Mama Theater, New York; *Company* published in New York.

1981   World premiere, 8 April, of *Rockaby,* performed by Billie Whitelaw at the Samuel Beckett Festival, State University of New York at Buffalo, directed by Alan Schneider; world premiere, 9 May, of *Ohio Impromptu,* performed by David Warrilow and Rand Mitchell at Ohio State University's Beckett Symposium, Columbus, directed by Alan Schneider—both premieres in honor of Beckett's seventy-fifth birthday; *Quad* televised 8 October, by SDR, directed by Beckett.

1982   World premiere, 21 July, of *Catastrophe,* at Avignon Festival, dedicated to Czech writer Vaclav Havel, directed by Stephan Meldbegg.

1983   Directs *Nacht und Traeume (Night and Dreams),* transmitted by SDR, 19 May; *What Where* performed at Graz Festival; *Worstward Ho* published in London and New York.

1984   Actors and Directors Theatre, at 410 West Forty-second Street, New York, renamed Samuel Beckett Theatre and opens with production of *Endgame,* directed by Alvin Epstein. San Quentin Drama Workshop production of *Waiting for Godot* presented in London, supervised by Beckett.

1986   Beckett's eightieth birthday celebrated with performances of his plays at festivals and conferences around the world.

1987   *Waiting for Godot* performed at National Theatre, London, directed by Michael Rudman and starring Alec McCowen and John Alderton.

1988   *Waiting for Godot* performed at Lincoln Center, New York, directed by Mike Nichols and starring Steve Martin and Robin Williams.

1989   Beckett's wife, Suzanne, dies in Paris, 17 July; Beckett dies of respiratory problems in Paris, 21 December, and on 26 December, is buried, after private funeral, at Montparnasse Cemetery.

LITERARY AND HISTORICAL CONTEXT

1

BACKGROUNDS AND INFLUENCES

Of the numerous influences on post–World War II European drama, perhaps the most significant were Antonin Artaud (1896–1948), Bertolt Brecht (1898–1956), and the French absurdists. Artaud was a tormented avant-gardist whose manifesto, *The Theater and Its Double* (1938), advocated a "theater of cruelty" returning to ancient rites, primitive rituals, and the nonverbal ceremonies of the Far East; Brecht, the German dramatist, tried "epic theater" to overthrow dramatic conventions and to challenge audiences to think rather than feel; and the French absurdists, as they were identified by critic Martin Esslin, in 1961, presented in existential terms the absurdity of the human condition, anywhere, anytime. Of these three influences, the last were the most influential, and of them the most outstanding was probably Samuel Beckett (1906–89).

Following World War II, existentialism as a philosophical viewpoint aroused considerable interest, especially through the essays and plays of Jean-Paul Sartre (1905–80). A philosopher and writer of fiction, Sartre turned to playwriting in 1943 with *The Flies,* ostensibly a modern adaptation of Aeschylus *The Libation Bearers,* but also an appeal to the French people to rise up against Nazi oppression. During the next 15 years, Sartre went on to write *No Exit* (1944), *The Respectable Prostitute* (1946), *Dirty Hands* (1948), *The Devil and the Good Lord* (1951), *Nekrassov* (1955), and *The Condemned of Altona* (1959), all of which dramatize his existential viewpoint: "Denying the existence of God, fixed standards of conduct, and verifiable moral codes, Sartre argues that each man must choose his own values and live by them regardless of prevailing standards, for to conform unquestioningly to the conventions established by others is the immoral response of a robot rather than the responsible act of a true being."[1]

The writings of another French philosopher, Albert Camus (1913–60), proved equally significant. Although Camus did write a few plays and stage adaptations, of which *Caligula* (1938) is by common consent his best, it was his essay "The Myth of Sisyphus" (1943), that had a major impact on contemporary drama by defining as it does the name and rationale of "absurdist": "A world that can be explained by reasoning, however faulty, is a familiar world. But in a universe that is suddenly deprived of illusions and of light, man feels a stranger. His is an irremediable exile, because he is deprived of memories of a lost homeland as much as he lacks the hope of a promised land to come. This divorce between man and his life, the actor and his setting, truly constitutes the feeling of Absurdity."[2] Although Camus did not identify himself as an existentialist, his conclusions were similar to Sartre's, and together, the two provided the philosophical foundation for the absurdist movement, which began to come into being in the early 1950s.

Of the French absurdists, Arthur Adamov (1908–70), Eugene Ionesco (b. 1912), Jean Genêt (1910–86), and Samuel Beckett (1906–89) have achieved major importance. The Russian-born Adamov began his literary career in Paris in the 1920s as a surrealist poet, withdrew from literature in the 1930s, and then turned to playwriting around 1945. His plays, *La Parodie* (1947) and *L'Invasion* (1948)—both concerned with the impossibility of communication—were finally staged in 1952 and 1950, respectively. These were followed by other plays also in the style of the theater of the absurd: *La Grande et la Petite Manoeuvre* (1950), *Professor Taranne* (1953), and

Le Ping-pong (1955), the last depicting life in terms of a pointless and interminable pinball-machine contest.

The Romanian-born Ionesco spent most of his childhood in Paris, his mother being French, then his early manhood in Romania, where he began writing while teaching French. In 1936, on his return to France, he wrote a series of one-act tragicomedies, *The Bald Soprano* (1948), *The Lesson* (1951), *Jack; or, The Submission* (1950), and *The Chairs* (1951), remaining among the most impressive examples of the entire theater of the absurd. In 1953, Ionesco turned to writing full-length plays, *Amédée; or, How to Get Rid of It* (1954), *The Killer* (1957), *Rhinoceros* (1958), and *Exit the King* (1961), to mention only a few. Recurrent themes in these plays are the breakdown of language, humanity's absurd vulnerability from the world without and the psychic world within, the proliferation of materialism, and the hysteria of mass conformity.

Ionesco's contemporary, Jean Genêt, was born and lived in France, where the notoriety of his private life earned him as much publicity as did his novels, poems, and plays. He was often sentenced to jail for theft, and when released his refuge was the homosexual underworld. It was in prison that he began writing poems and fiction in the early 1940s, and then his first play in 1947—*Deathwatch,* a long one-act, concerning the conflicts, personal and erotic, among three handsome prison inmates. Other plays followed: *The Maids* (1947), *The Balcony* (1957), *The Blacks* (1959), and *The Screens* (1966), each in its own way dealing with acts of ceremony, dream, and masquerade in which everyday realities are replaced by "absurd" illusions or impersonations, perhaps no more incredible and unconvincing that the realities they supplant. Whereas Adamov and Ionesco stress in their respective ways the importance of human relationships both personal and social, Genêt, who viewed "all systems of value as entirely arbitrary, transform[ed] life into a series of ceremonies and rituals which give an air of stability and importance to otherwise nonsensical behavior" (Brockett, 650). Beckett, however, dubbed by his biographer Deirdre Bair the "spokesman for disenchanted men,"[3] seemed more concerned with the position and plight of humanity in the overall scheme of existence and its remarkable stamina to struggle on, often without a sense of either direction or purpose.

Irish-born Beckett visited Paris for the first time in 1928, moving there permanently in 1937. Initially a novelist, he turned to playwriting in 1953 and wrote *En attendant Godot* (*Waiting for Godot*). Performed in Paris that same year, *Godot* was soon performed around the world, almost instantly and unexpectedly (particularly to its author) successful. *Godot*'s success is considered by many the first major triumph of the absurdist movement and the beginning of a genuine popular awareness of the theater of the absurd.

One of the cornerstones of the theater of the absurd, *Waiting for Godot* is a two-act tragicomedy about two old men who faithfully await the rumored arrival of an elusive Godot who will rescue them in some undefined way from their desperate circumstances, but who actually never appears. Vladimir and Estragon, the play's protagonists, are constantly torn about whether to leave or to stay waiting for a Godot who may or may never arrive.

Endgame, which Beckett wrote some four years later, takes this struggle to the ultimate. Its protagonists, Hamm and Clov, bound in master-servant symbiosis, struggle with the purpose of going on at all. In his desperate requests for time killers as well as painkillers (ultimately death), Hamm questions the struggle of continuing to live, inevitably distracting himself from final decision by inventive schemes and devices of self-dramatization that enable him to tolerate another day. His servant, Clov, on the other hand, exercises his love-hate relationship with Hamm by dutiful performance of daily routine activities as he struggles with his dilemma of whether to stay with the overbearing and dependent Hamm or leave and take his chances at survival in the "outer hell" that may exist outside their known shelter.

Endgame is perhaps Beckett's most representative play and his purest dramatic statement of the timeless and universal human condition; even more than *Godot,* it presents one of Beckett's most distilled and highly charged depictions of the postwar human dilemma. As Oscar G. Brockett has observed, "Probably more than any other writer, Beckett expressed the postwar doubts about man's capacity to understand and control his world" (Brockett, 650). In a *New York*

Times (19 August 1984) interview with Beckett, critic Rosette Lamont concluded that Beckett is one of the preeminent classical writers of our time as well as a post-Holocaust author, "deeply marked by the horrors of our age. . . . [His] plays, despite the surface of absurdism, are an amalgam of politics, morality and metaphysics. [His] early avant-garde identity was a mask, imposed on [him] by others. [He] stand[s] revealed today, [a] great [humanist, a voice] which proclaim[s] those values that make us human."[4]

2

THE IMPORTANCE OF ENDGAME

It was through his plays rather than his fiction that Samuel Beckett became internationally known as one of the most distinguished and disturbing writers of this century. Although his first play, *Eleutheria* (1948), remains unpublished and unperformed and his second play, *En attendant Godot,* or *Waiting for Godot* (1953), has become a world-acclaimed masterpiece, it is his third play, *Fin de partie,* or *Endgame* (1957), that many consider his greatest single work. It is *Endgame,* probably less often performed on the stage or studied in the classroom than *Godot,* that critic Herbert Blau has dubbed the "most profound drama in the modern theater"[1] because it addresses the "great mystique of modern helplessness [and thereby provides] us, exploring the rubble, with the most compelling theatrical image of the courage to be" (Gontarski, 261). Ruby Cohn, one of Beckett's most perceptive critics, describes *Endgame* as presenting "the death of the stock props of Western civilization—family cohesion, filial devotion, parental and connubial love, faith in God, empirical knowledge, and artistic creation,"[2] and so identifies the major themes not only of this remarkable play, but also of Beckett's work in general.

The Importance of Endgame

Of all his works, Beckett himself considered *Endgame* his favorite or preferred play, pairing it with his novel *The Unnamable* (1950) as work whose composition gave him the most personal satisfaction. Depicting as it does the persistent struggle of its two decrepit protagonists to live with a kind of stoicism while scrutinizing the bleak landscape for some shred of hope, *Endgame* dramatizes the final words of *The Unnamable:* "You must go on, I can't go on, I'll go on." It heralds the dictum Beckett was to repeat in *Worstward Ho* (1983), one of his last works of fiction: "Try again. Fail again. Fail better."

Deirdre Bair, Beckett's biographer, has suggested that in *Endgame,* Beckett "had consciously set out to write a play that would not only set forth a cogent representation of his view of humanity and life, but one that would be a careful, artfully constructed theatrical vehicle" (Bair, 479). He dedicated *Endgame* to Roger Blin, the prominent French director and actor, who, with French actor Jean Martin, had inspired it, and sent Blin a typed copy of the completed manuscript with the following note: "For you, if you really want it, but only if you really want it. Because it really has meaning, the others are only everyday" (Bair, 479).

A stark drama in one act, *Endgame* concerns two decrepit protagonists—the blind, paralyzed Hamm and his lame, fetch-and-carry servant, Clov—who manage to eke out their remaining days in a tomb-like shelter encompassed by a genocidal world, while Hamm's elderly and legless parents, Nagg and Nell, are slowly dying in two ashbins nearby. Despite its grim subject matter, *Endgame*'s bleak vision is mitigated by the characters' occasional, and striking, revelations of ironic humor and human compassion toward each other and their circumstances throughout the entirety of the play's action.

When Beckett directed *Endgame* in Paris in 1964 (Patrick Magee playing Hamm and Jack MacGowran playing Clov), his directorial approach to the play stressed its concern with human interdependency: "that man must depend upon his fellowman in some way no matter how awful; [hence, the] love-hate relationship between Hamm and Clov that exists right through the play" (Gontarski, 218). Jack MacGowran, when interviewed by Richard Toscan in 1973, also commented that Beckett's concern is, above all, "human distress, not human despair" (Gontarski, 215) and that *Endgame* is perhaps Beckett's harshest and most tragic play because the moonscape "world upon which Clov [looks], through the [shelter] window[s, is one] devoid of anything, any human living being" (Gontarski, 217).

In response to theater critics' nervous rash of commentary following the play's first French performance, Beckett wrote to Alan Schneider, the American director of *Endgame:*

> When it comes to journalists, I feel the only line is to refuse to be involved with exegesis of any kind. And to insist on the extreme simplicity of dramatic situation and issue. If that's not enough for them, and it obviously isn't, it's plenty for us, and we have no elucidations to offer of mysteries that are all of their making. My work is a matter of fundamental sounds (no joke intended) made as fully as possible, and I accept responsibility for nothing else. If people want to have headaches among the overtones, let them. And provide their own aspirin. Hamm as stated, and Clov as stated, *nec tecum nec sine te,* in such a play, and in such a world, that's all I can manage, more than I could.[3]

Endgame, not itself squeamish, is not meant to comfort the squeamish, whether directors, actors, or audience. Part of Beckett's compassion being erasure of illusion, he invites us in *Endgame* to recognize our day-by-day struggles against varying degrees of confusion, fear, helplessness, and despair, often a bitter pill for a public to swallow.

3

ENDGAME'S CRITICAL RECEPTION

When *Fin de partie* (the original French version of *Endgame*) opened at the Royal Court Theatre, London, on 3 April 1957, the theater critics, with the possible exception of Harold Hobson (Beckett's staunchest defender as well as most perceptive commentator), were at a loss as to how to respond to the play. Kenneth Tynan, in his *Observer* review (7 April 1957), responded strongly: "[Beckett's] new play . . . makes it clear that his purpose is neither to move nor to help us. For him, man is a pygmy who connives at his own inevitable degradation. There, says Beckett, stamping on the face of mankind: there, that is how life is."[1]

When the play opened in Paris three weeks later at the intimate Studio des Champs-Élysées on 26 April, the French theater critics (whose patriotic spirit had been offended at the thought of a French play receiving its premiere in England) welcomed it with little enthusiasm. The two most favorable critics, A. J. Leventhal and Maurice Nadeau, both based their reviews on their readings of the already published text, rather than on their experience of seeing the play actually performed. Leventhal did predict, however, that "*Fin de partie* cannot hope for the same success that attended *En attendant Godot* [*Waiting*

11

for Godot]. . . . [A]n audience, faced with uttermost pain on the stage, is likely to wilt at the experience, though it may well be a catharsis for such who have hitherto refused in their euphoria to look beyond their optimistic noses."[2]

For several months subsequent to the London and Paris premieres of *Fin de partie,* Beckett devoted himself painstakingly to its English translation, entitled *Endgame;* this first English production, directed by Alan Schneider, opened at the Cherry Lane Theatre, New York, on 28 January 1958. The English version of the play received much attention from theater reviewers, and John Unterecker, recalling its New York opening more than a year later, regarded it as "a significant off-Broadway success."[3] Alan Schneider, the play's director, was, however, skeptical about the critics' appreciation of Beckett's artistic achievement in *Endgame:* "Beckett is that most uncompromised of men, one who writes—and lives—as he must, and not as the world— and the world's critics—want him to. [He is] an artist, who works with no fears of 'failure,' which has fed him most of his writing life, or any expectation of 'success,' which has only lately greeted him."[4]

When *Endgame* in English was presented at the Royal Court Theatre, London (October 1958), its successful production was staged by George Devine, who also played the role of Hamm. Since then, it has been staged variously. Its most recent production was in New York's newly named Samuel Beckett Theatre in 1984. There its controversial off-Broadway revival was directed by Alvin Epstein, who also played Hamm and who chose to stage the play on what appeared to be the underground platform of a New York subway station, rather than in the bare, cell-like setting that Beckett has specified in his stage directions. (Other experimental settings in which *Endgame* has been performed include a chicken-wire cage, a boxing arena, an infant's playpen, and the semblance of the inside of a human skull.) The play has also been transformed into opera, modern dance, and a comic farce heavily laced with American slang. Despite the author's explicit stage directions, who knows what the future will mean to production of Beckett's remarkable play?

Endgame has already become the subject of much critical speculation. Bell Gale Chevigny, in her introduction to *Twentieth Century*

Interpretations of Endgame (a collection of eight significant critics'
analyses of the play), offers a range of other possible readings, all of
which "may be regarded as part of a general enterprise to find the
main drift of life by going to life's perimeters."[5] To Chevigny,
"Beckett's obsession with the illusion of life and the elusiveness of
being, made brilliantly dramatic in *Endgame,* are historically tied to
the conditions of theatre at their most profound" (Chevigny, 7). As
audience members, Chevigny suggests, "we identify with a character
on the stage more than in other arts, but we always know him [or her]
for an actor who reads an invisible script. Thus our belief and our
skepticism are deeply engaged at once—a condition which is shared by
Beckett the author and his creatures" (Chevigny, 7).

Further, *Endgame,* Chevigny suggests, can be seen as "a tool by
which the losses of contemporary life may be assessed. . . . [By attack-
ing] the [conventional] meaning[s] of objectivity and subjectivity,
Beckett exposes the bankrupt assumptions of rationality itself, . . .
[thus posing] the fiercest challenge to everything by which we try to
live" (Chevigny, 12–13).

In the chapter on Beckett entitled "The Search for the Self" in his
The Theatre of the Absurd (1961), Martin Esslin credits the suggestion
that *Endgame* is a monodrama dealing with death and dying:

> The enclosed space with the two tiny windows through which
> Clov observes the outside world; the [ashbins] that hold the sup-
> pressed and despised parents, and whose lids Clov is ordered to
> press down when they become obnoxious; Hamm, blind and
> emotional; Clov, performing the function of the senses for him—
> all these might well represent different aspects of a single person-
> ality, repressed memories in the subconscious mind, the emotional
> and the intellectual selves. Is Clov then the intellect, bound to
> serve the emotions, instincts, and appetites, and trying to free
> himself from such disorderly and tyrannical masters, yet doomed
> to die when its connection with the animal side of the personality
> is severed? Is the death of the outside world the gradual receding
> of the links to reality that take place in the process of aging and
> dying? Is *Endgame* a monodrama depicting the dissolution of a
> personality in the hour of death?[6]

Richard M. Goldman, in his essay "*Endgame* and Its Score-keepers," describes the many attempts at criticism of the play as "beautiful failures. . . . For we need to determine what kind of art Beckett is practising rather than translating his works into a set of meanings or placing them along the continuum of literary history" (Chevigny, 33). In *Samuel Beckett: The Comic Gamut* (1962), Ruby Cohn sees Clov, Hamm, and Nagg as three generations as well as three stages of physical decomposition. Like Malone in Beckett's trilogy, it is Hamm, the middle member, Cohn suggests, "who is at the height (such as it is) of his creative powers. But as the focus of *Endgame* narrows to the Hamm-Clov relationship, the tension is tautened between the creator and creature until, finally, after the end of the play as played, one is (perhaps) replaced by the other, and the whole absurd, heartbreaking cycle begins again" (Cohn 1962, 242). Further, Cohn suggests, "Resurrection into another and reduced life, into another and slower death, may take place—if at all—only through the play of creation" (Cohn 1962, 242).

In his critical study of Beckett, Hugh Kenner's perceptive commentary on *Endgame* is entitled "Life in the Box." Not only does Kenner suggest that the play's setting may be the inside of an immense human skull and the play's opening action plainly a metaphor for waking up, but he also affirms what Beckett called in a letter to director Alan Schneider "the power of the text to claw."[7] He further suggests that *Endgame* "strikes, however, its unique precarious balance between rage and art, immobilizing all characters but one, rotating before us for ninety unbroken minutes the surfaces of Nothing, always designedly faltering on the brink of utter insignificance: theater reduced to its elements in order that theatricalism may explore without mediation its own boundaries: a bleak unforgettable tour de force and probably its author's single most remarkable work."[8] Antony Easthope, in his essay "Hamm, Clov, and Dramatic Method in *Endgame*" (which first appeared in *Modern Drama*), analyzes Hamm's character as well as the relationship between Hamm and Clov, and then explores the dramatic tension created in the play by Beckett's juxtaposing a formal conversational surface with serious, often terrifying depths.

Endgame's Reception

In his "Approach to *Endgame*," published originally in French in *Studi Francesi* 33 (January–April 1967), Ross Chambers analyzes the dramatic elements of time and space in the play. To Chambers, the characters in *Endgame* are in a real sense at the end of their rope:

> [T]hey have reached the unending end of a long existence already filled with action and words, so it is not surprising that they should be weary, and especially that they should have run out of inspiration. Unable to find new words, new gestures, they are reduced to repeating indefinitely the things they have done and said many times before. Their life is not unlike Hamm's story which he is able to "get on with," "in spite of everything," but which appears at one and the same time to be hopelessly bogged down in repetition and frighteningly near its conclusion. (Chevigny, 77–78)

Theodor W. Adorno, in his essay entitled "Towards an Understanding of *Endgame*," translated by Samuel Weber, probes the play's dramatic situation, characters, and setting, as well as its plot, language, humor, form, themes, and concerns with time, history, and identity, via references to Brecht, Eliot, Heidegger, Husserl, Ibsen, Joyce, Kierkegaard, Lukács, Mann, Proust, and Sartre. Also provocative is George E. Wellwarth's commentary on Beckett and particularly *Endgame* in *The Theater of Protest and Paradox* (1972). To Wellwarth, "Beckett is the prophet of negation and sterility [who] holds out no hope to humanity, only a picture of unrelieved blackness; and those who profess to see in Beckett signs of a Christian approach or signs of compassion are simply refusing to see what is there."[9] Regarding *Endgame* in particular, Wellwarth contends that it dramatizes, through its chess-game allegory, Beckett's belief in the utter futility of any human attempt to arrive at a conclusion about anything.

By 1973, various productions of *Endgame* prompted Harold Hobson, one of Beckett's most perceptive commentators, to write, "In recent years there has been some danger of Mr. Beckett's being sentimentalized. Self-defensively we are driven to persuade ourselves that his plays are not really filled with terror and horror, but are, at bottom, jolly good fun. Well, they are not jolly good fun. They are amongst the most frightening prophecies of, and longing for, doom ever written."[10] And so the elusive nature of Beckett's *Endgame* continues to inspire critical imagination, to say nothing of scholarly brilliance in support of its own salary and professional advancement. As Beckett acknowledged to Alan Schneider, *Endgame* is a difficult play to "get right." But despite the initial antagonistic response of theater critics, an effective production of the play can, as Tom Bishop suggests in the *Beckett Circle* (Spring 1980), "elevate [it] to its proper tragic stature without sacrificing its corrosive, brilliant black comic values."[11]

A READING

4

A STRUCTURAL ANALYSIS

So much has been conjectured about the meaning of *Fin de partie,* or *Endgame,* that anyone writing about it automatically becomes a participant in an international critical debate continuous since the play's London premiere in French in 1957. Although Beckett himself customarily maintained a guarded silence about the "meaning" of his work, he did, in the case of *Endgame,* make at least two public statements demanding careful note. Critic Ruby Cohn, in *Back to Beckett* (1973), has documented Beckett's statement: "There are no accidents in *Fin de partie.* Everything is based on analogy and repetition."[1] Moreover, according to Beckett's biographer, Deirdre Bair, "When Beckett told some English-speaking friends that he had written a play called *Fin de partie,* they translated it as 'End of the game.' 'No,' Beckett replied emphatically. 'It is *Endgame,* as in chess'" (Bair, 467). Bair also notes that critical explication of *Endgame* is generally facilitated by recognition of chess as the play's controlling metaphor: "In keeping with the chess analogy, everything in this play is balanced, and each movement, action or speech depends on another. . . . A line of tragedy is often followed by one of comedy. There is pathos undercut by bathos. It is a play within a play; Hamm and Clov realize they are actors, that dialogue keeps them upon the stage; at times they fear the introduction of subplots, at others they speak of asides" (Bair, 467). Also, Bair notes, in *Endgame,* "For every story that is told, there is an appropriate response. Clov draws back the curtains, first on one window, then on the other, in an identical repetition of the action. The list of moves, countermoves and responsive moves does not . . . end here, but these are enough to demonstrate the point" (Bair, 467).

Beckett, through his deliberate use of chess as *Endgame*'s controlling metaphor, not only reinforces the play's overall spirit of timeless universality and cosmopolitanism but also heightens the dramatic significance of the inventive stratagems and tactics both Hamm and Clov contrive to carry on their interminable, daily games of master-servant survival. Chess, the most cosmopolitan of games, derives its name from the Persian word *shah,* meaning "king," the name of one of the principal chessmen or types of pieces used in the game. Although the origin of chess has been lost in obscurity, its invention has been variously ascribed to the Greeks, Romans, Babylonians, Scythians, Egyptians, Jews, Persians, Chinese, Hindus, Arabians, Araucanians (members of a linguistic stock of South American Indians of Chile and the Argentine pampas), Castilians, Irish, and Welsh. Some scholars have even endeavored to attribute its origin to specific individuals, such as Japheth (the youngest of Noah's three sons), Shem (the eldest of Noah's three sons and the traditional ancestor of the Semitic people), King Solomon (the son of David and the king of Israel in the tenth century B.C.), the philosopher Xerxes, the Greek chieftain Palamedes, Aristotle, Attalus (who died circa 200 B.C.), the mandarin Hansing, the Brahman Sissa, and Shatrenscha, who was said to be a celebrated Persian astronomer. Many of these ascriptions are of doubtful authenticity, others are based on meager evidence, and some have been the result of easily traceable errors. Nonetheless, it was not until the thirteenth century A.D. that we hear of checkered chessboards being used in Europe; formerly, they were uncolored.

Once known as "checkers," chess is a game of skill played by two opponents with certain chessmen or types of pieces on a special board divided into 64 checkered squares of two alternating colors. As a mere pastime, chess can be easily learned, and with a moderate amount of study, a person can become a fair player, but the higher degrees of chess skill can be attained only by extensive study and diligent effort. The expert player or "master" must not only grasp the subtle variations in which the game abounds, but also be able to apply that knowledge in the face of opposition and to summon up, as occasion demands, all the foresight, brilliance, and ingenuity the player can muster, both in attack and in defense. Two chess players competing over the board may be likened to two military leaders encountering each other on the battlefield, the strategy and the tactics being not dissimilar in spirit.

Each side (white or black) has 16 chessmen or pieces: a king, a queen, two rooks (or castles), two bishops, and two knights that occupy the back line. The eight chessmen occupying the front line are called pawns. Each chessman is moved according to specific rules, and is removed from the board when it is displaced (or "captured") by the move of one of the opposing chessmen into its square. Hamm, Clov, and the aging Nagg and Nell have been viewed by many as king, knight, and pawns, respectively, struggling to survive in the final phase or endgame of a metaphoric human chess game of life. The king (Hamm) has the power to move in any direction, but only one square at a time, except in castling, and cannot capture any opponent's piece that is protected by another. The knight (Clov) has the power to move from one corner of any rectangle of three squares by two to the opposite corner, and it is no obstacle to the knight's move if the intervening squares are occupied. The pawns (Nagg and Nell), for their first move, each have the power to advance either one or two squares straight forward, but afterward one square only, and this whether on starting, each exercised its privilege of moving two squares or not. A pawn can never move backward, and it can capture another piece only by moving diagonally—one square to its right or left front. When a pawn arrives, however, at the eighth square (at the extreme limit of the board), it must be exchanged for another piece of the same color, so that the player may, for example, have two or more queens on the board at one time.

In chess, the king can never be captured, but when any piece or pawn attacks him, he is said to be "in check," and the fact of his being so attacked should be acknowledged by the opposing player saying "check," whereupon the king must move from the square he occupies, or be protected from check by the interposition of one of his own men, or the attacking piece must be captured. If, however, when the king is in check, none of these things can be done, it is "checkmate" (in Persian, *shah mat,* meaning "the king is dead"), known generally as "mate," whereupon the game is over, the player whose king has been thus checkmated being the loser. When a king is not in check, but his player has no move left except one that would place the king in check, it is "stalemate," and the game is a draw.

As a whole, a game of chess consists of three parts or stages: the opening, the middle, and the endgame. The last stage is reached when the opponents, as a result of the prolonged battle, are so reduced in number of pieces that the kings themselves must take the field. The endgame, having its own distinctive laws in which the value of pieces undergoes a considerable change, requires much special study in its own right. The kings, for example, leave their passive role and become attacking forces. The pawns increase in value, while that of some of the other pieces may, in certain cases, diminish. Two knights, for example, without pawns, become virtually valueless, as no checkmate can be effected with them, if the opponent plays correctly. In the majority of cases, however, the players must be guided by general principles, as the standard examples do not meet all cases.

Based on her research findings, Deirdre Bair feels certain that any critical explication of *Endgame* must include some acknowledgment of the influence of the French painter Marcel Duchamp (1887–1968). A formidable chess expert as well as an acquaintance of Beckett throughout the 1930s, Duchamp frequented, as did Beckett, the same Paris cafés where the best chess players gathered, and he occasionally wrote a chess column, which Beckett read with interest, for the Paris daily newspaper *Ce Soir.* In his *Complete Works* (posthumously published in 1970), Duchamp wrote, "Chess is a . . . violent sport . . . that does imply artistic connotations in the actual geometric patterns and variations of the actual setup of the pieces and in the combinative, tactical, strategical, and positional sense. It's a sad expression though—somewhat like religious art—it is not very gay. If it is anything, it is a struggle."[2]

A Structural Analysis

In 1932, Duchamp coauthored (with Halberstadt) a major work of chess literature, *Opposition and Sister Squares Are Reconciled,* which Beckett knew well. This book specifically concerns the third and final phase of a chess game, the endgame, which Deirdre Bair describes as follows:

> Generally speaking, a chess game has three parts: first is the opening, in which pieces are brought out and strategies instigated. In the next section, or middle game, the two opponents organize their moves. In the last part, the endgame, there is either a conversion of the advantage into a win, or else an attempt to nullify the disadvantage incurred in the middle game—also in search of the win. Usually in the endgame, there are no longer enough pieces left on the board to initiate an attack upon the king. This is when both kings are free to come to the center of the board, to confront each other, seemingly uncaring, as they execute the few limited moves still possible. (Bair, 465–66)

Bair notes two analyses of Duchamp's book that are especially relevant to Beckett's play. Pierre de Mossot, one of the first critics to review Duchamp's book, noted its particular concern with that crucial stage of the endgame in chess when most of the pieces have been lost, and only the kings and a few pawns remain on the board. "This special 'lone-pawns' situation," de Mossot further noted, "is treated only for the even more particular situation in which the pawns have been blocked and only the Kings can play. . . . Only certain moves and in limited number are possible. . . . The authors [Duchamp and Halberstadt] are the first to have noticed the synchronization of the moves of the Black King and the White King" (Bair, 466).

Another critic, Henri-Pierre Roché, described the gist of Duchamp's book as follows: "There comes a time toward the end of the game when there is almost nothing left on the board, and when the outcome depends on the fact that the King has a choice between two moves and may act in such a way as to suggest he has completely lost interest in winning the game. Then the other King, if he too is a true sovereign, can give the appearance of being even less interested, and so on" (Bair, 466). Moreover, Roché observed, the two kings can thus "waltz carelessly one by one across the board as though they weren't at all engaged in mortal combat. However, there are rules governing each step they take and the slightest mistake is instantly fatal. One must provoke the other to commit that blunder and keep his head at all times. These are the rules that Duchamp brought to light (the free and forbidden squares) all to amplify this haughty junket of the Kings" (Bair, 466).

Beckett himself has made certain statements about *Endgame* that seem to support both de Mossot's and Roché's analyses of Duchamp's book. In 1967, for example, when Beckett directed *Endspiel* (the German version of *Endgame*) in Berlin, he remarked to Ernst Schroeder, the German actor playing Hamm, that "Hamm is a king in this chess game lost from the start [who] . . . is only trying to delay the inevitable end" (Cohn 1973, 152).

Just as in *Endgame* the chess metaphor is literal and evident, chess appears figuratively relevant in many of Beckett's plays. To Beckett, writing—whether poetry, fiction, or drama—is a means by which "a person creates his own world, *un univers á part,* to withdraw [to] when one gets tired [and wishes] to get away from the chaos into a simpler world. . . . Now it is no longer possible to know everything, the tie between the self and things no longer exists. . . . One must make a world of one's own in order to satisfy one's need to know, to understand, one's need for order. . . . There, for me, lies the value of theatre. One turns out a small world with its own laws, conducts the actions as if upon a chess board."[3]

But many other symbols evident in *Endgame* invite equally cogent interpretations. J. W. Lambert, sees "a toppled Prospero"[4]; other critics, a King Lear, Hamlet, Noah and his ark, Beckett in Ireland, or even Beckett and his wife, Suzanne, in Roussillon, to mention only a few. The play's setting, with its two curtained window-eyes high up on the back wall looking out on sea and land, has been interpreted by critic Hugh Kenner as the interior of a human skull, and by others as a post-Armaggedon bomb shelter, protecting the last remaining human survivors on earth. By some, Hamm has been dubbed "James Joyce" or possibly even Beckett's father, and Clov as Beckett the Joycean disciple, or Beckett the son. In short, the range of interpretations of this enigmatic play is as varied as the fertile workings of the critical minds that have engaged with it. Beckett himself chose to remain detached and noncommittal about such conjectures. What personally interested him was the "shape" of ideas and sentences: "I take no sides. I am interested in the shape of ideas. There is a wonderful sentence in [Saint] Augustine: 'Do not despair; one of the thieves was saved. Do not presume; one of the thieves was damned.' That sentence has a wonderful shape. It is the shape that matters" (Schneider, 3).

Although Beckett personally assisted directors in four production of *Endgame*—the French premiere of *Fin de partie* in London (1957), the Paris-London production in English (1964), the German *Endspiel* in Berlin (1967), and the Royal Court London "Beckett Season" production (1976)—it was not until 1967, when he staged it in German translation by Elmar Tophoven in Berlin for the Schiller-Theater Werkstatt, that his name actually appeared as director of his work in a theater program. Until this point in his career, Beckett had been willing to entrust the ultimate responsibility for staging his plays to others, apparently with growing misgivings. By 1962, he had begun to articulate his personal directorial position in conversation with Charles Marowitz: "[Stage directors] don't seem to have any sense of form in movement. The kind of form one finds in music, for instance, where themes keep recurring. When in a text, actions are repeated, they ought to be made unusual the first time, so that when they happen again—in exactly the same way—an audience will recognize them from before."[5]

Beckett, as director as well as author, had very definite ideas about how he wanted *Endgame* staged and acted, down to the smallest detail, and he clearly regarded his play as having a "closed system" to be perfected for its own sake. He did not want the actors in any way to cater or "play to" the audience in their performances, and his own directing of the play seemed, like the writing itself, designed not to win audience approval but rather to be an end in itself for him personally (McMillan and Fehsenfeld, 220). Patrick Magee, who played Hamm in a 1964 London production of *Endgame* directed by Michael Blake and supervised by Beckett, confirms the difficult challenge this play poses for actors: "You can't do tricks in this play. No, not in this one. It won't stand rubbishy acting, the tricks" (McMillan and Fehsenfeld, 181).

When Beckett staged *Endspiel* in Berlin in 1967, his directing followed a "guiding principle which one would have believed alien to the dramatic stage: a decided split between action and speech. As though he were delivering a course in mechanics, he lectures—'Never let your changes of position and voice come together. First comes (a) the altered bodily stance; after it, following a slight pause, comes (b) the corresponding utterance'" (McMillan, 211). He also wanted as much laughter as possible from the characters onstage, for he considered *Endgame* "a playful piece" (McMillan and Fehsenfeld, 218). His purpose was to make credible to an audience Hamm's statement to Clov "Ah great fun we had, the two of us, great fun" (McMillan and Fehsenfeld, 218). Beckett also suggested to his German actors that *Endgame* could be likened to " 'fire and ashes': the antagonism between the characters flares up and subsides and flares again" (McMillan and Fehsenfeld, 201), similar to "a burnt-out hearth from which flames break out from time to time, to sink back again into the ashes" (McMillan and Fehsenfeld, 238). So, too, did Beckett's directing of *Endspiel* in Berlin confirm what critic Hugh Kenner observes about Hamm and Clov's adversarial relationship: that they "confront each other as king and knight of an imaginary chess match" (McMillan and Fehsenfeld, 223). When asked, however, by one of the German cast members if this chess analogy could be extended to include Nagg and Nell as well, Beckett was unwilling to extend the chess comparison that far.

For the 1967 Berlin production of *Endspiel*, Beckett had prepared a director's notebook to provide a detailed running account of the play's action, stage directions for specific actions or bits of stage "business" the actors might perform when delivering each line of dialogue, and perhaps even more importantly, a highly instructive breakdown of the script into 16 sections or movements:

1. Clov's mime-show and first soliloquy.
2. Hamm's wakening, first soliloquy, and first [verbal exchange] with Clov.
3. Dialogue, Nagg and Nell.

4. Dialogue between Hamm and Clov including the "little turn—round the world!" and ending with Clov's ah-me, "If I could kill him . . ."
5. Clov's "comedy" with ladder and telescope.
6. Hamm's interrogation of Clov, rising to the burlesque flea scene.
7. Dialogue between Hamm and Clov, ending with the ironic mirror image of the [toy-] dog episode.
8. Clov's rebellion, leading [up to] Hamm's story of the madman and trailing off into the alarm clock scene.
9. Hamm's story of the beggar.
10. The prayer, ending with Nagg's curse.
11. Hamm's and Clov's play within a play: Hamm's chronicle.
12. The second turn with the chair.
13. Dialogue between Hamm and Clov, leading [up to]:
14. Hamm's [self-defined] role.
15. Emancipation of Clov, [indicated by] his monologue and exit.
16. Hamm's final monologue. (McMillan and Fehsenfeld, 206)

In addition to serving as a road map to actors in rehearsal, this 16-section breakdown indicates a very helpful structural analysis of *Endgame*, reflecting Beckett's own concept of his play's structure "based upon a carefully balanced set of theatrical beginnings and endings and a cumulative set of prayers, prophecies, and curses organising the action leading to Hamm's final isolation as his calls to Clov remain unanswered" (McMillan and Fehsenfeld, 187–88). This structural concept also reveals that "In the centre and then interspersed as a counter theme or subplot indicating the possibility of a new beginning is Hamm's story of the boy and his father" (McMillan and Fehsenfeld, 188).

Although both *Fin de partie* and *Endgame* have been internationally produced by such major directors as Roger Blin, George Devine, and Alan Schneider, none of those versions of the play enjoyed a fraction of the success of *Waiting for Godot*, produced four years earlier. To speculate on this discrepancy in popularity: it may be due in part to the fact that *Endgame*'s disturbing vision and static dramatic situation present too unsettling an experience for both recent directors and theatergoers seeking safely diverting and amusing entertainment. But whatever the explanation, this unfortunate discrepancy may explain

Beckett's interest in personally directing *Endgame*—which he preferred to *Godot*—whenever possible during the latter part of his life.
As a result, Beckett's own directorial analysis and scene breakdown of
the play are well documented by others, becoming a significant contri-
bution to Beckett scholarship in general. Beckett's own 16-section
breakdown—combined with his rehearsal directions and comments to
his actors, as scrupulously documented in *Back to Beckett* (1973) and
Just Play: Beckett's Theater (1980), by Ruby Cohn, and *Beckett in the
Theatre: The Author as Practical Playwright and Director,* volume 1
(1988), by Dougald McMillan and Martha Fehsenfeld—generates the
rationale of the following dramatic analysis of *Endgame*.

SECTION 1

Section 1 establishes the essential tableau or pictorial scene of the
play: stage setting, furniture, and characters with which it opens and
with which, in section 16, it symmetrically ends. The setting (which is
bathed in a peculiar gray light throughout the action) is the sparsely
furnished interior of a tomblike shelter or tower whose two narrow,
high-set windows, facing earth and sea, respectively, are curtained.
Downstage left is a narrow slit of a door opening to the outside world
as well as to the private kingdom of the servant Clov, his kitchen. On
the wall near the door is a picture, its face turned to the wall, possibly
as a sign of grief or mourning. In the center of the room and covered
by an old sheet, the blind and paralyzed Hamm sits motionless in an
armchair on castors. Downstage right and close to each other are two
dirty and battered ashbins, also covered with an old sheet. Clov,
Hamm's servant, stands motionless by the door, his eyes riveted on his
sleeping master.

After taking a brief pause, Clov moves, in a stiff, staggering manner, from his stance by the door and begins (with the aid of a stepladder) his daily "inspection" or ritual unveiling, drawing back the
curtains on both windows, observing through each (first the sea window and then the earth window) the dubious prospects of the waste-

land without, then unsheeting and uncovering the two ashbins, like furniture in a closed house, to inspect their separate contents, and last unsheeting Hamm, who is garbed in a dressing gown, a stiff toque (a modification of a sixteenth-century, close-fitting, plumed hat), and thick woolen socks. Hamm's other covers are a lap rug on his knees, a whistle (his instrument of control) hanging from his neck, and a large blood-stained handkerchief (Hamm's "old stancher") over his face.

Observing that his master seems to be still asleep, Clov heads for the door and (presumably) the logic and order of his 10-by-10-by-10-foot kitchen refuge. But then he halts, turns toward the auditorium, and delivers, in a toneless manner, the play's opening soliloquy, "Finished, it's finished, nearly finished, it must be nearly finished,"[6] establishing the play's major theme or concern with the need to bring matters (presumably life) to some reasonable closure or ending. Clov's seeming preoccupation with "finishing" matters may also aptly allude to Christ's death on the cross: "When Jesus therefore had received the vinegar, he said, It is finished: and he bowed his head, and gave up the ghost" (John 19:30). The question becomes, however, For whom is Clov really performing his soliloquy—the sleeping Hamm, the audience, or himself? Or is he merely parroting here the words and sentiments he has heard his master, Hamm, so frequently and routinely utter? Clov then remarks on an "impossible heap" of grain that grows, grain by grain, imperceptibly larger each day. Beckett's reference here is to Eubulides of Miletus, the fourth-century B.C. Greek philosopher and inventor of logical paradoxes, who wrote, "One grain of corn is not a heap. Add a grain and there is yet no heap. When does a heap begin?" This "grain-of-time" theme, Ruby Cohn suggests, reinforces the constant opposition present in the play between the inability to end with the need to bring matters to an ending. Though Hamm and Clov may spend their days wondering about this puzzling question, their action denies the possibility of change: "Each word, each event, is another grain, but the grains never mount up to the impossible heap of infinity" (Cohn 1973, 144).

Clov's next statement, "I can't be punished any more" (*EG*, 1), not only reinforces his feelings of discontent with his present servitude but also expresses his heightened desire to leave Hamm altogether and take his chances in the world outside. Clov concludes his soliloquy with a description of his nicely proportioned kitchen, where he will now go to await Hamm's waking whistle-call.

Consistently throughout section 1, Clov's deliberation in performing his daily inspection conveys to the audience in some immediate way that something is wrong or, at least, out of the ordinary on this particular day. Further, in his opening inspection, Clov brings every object within the shelter into the action by his "looking" at each carefully, in a deliberate way. In checking to see whether anything has changed, he makes certain that nothing has (McMillan and Fehsenfeld, 208). Like Hamm, he has a need for order, and his conscientious performance of his routine inspection is one of its manifestations. In section 11, he actually articulates it: "I love order. It's my dream. A world where all would be silent and still and each thing in its last place, under the last dust" (*EG*, 57).

Clov shares several significant affinities with Pozzo's old and faithful servant, Lucky, in *Waiting for Godot*. Like Lucky, Clov is also dubiously "lucky," in that he too is defined by his servitude to his master, Hamm. Clov's daily agenda of routine activities and tasks provides him with a predictable structure and purpose to his days, and at the same time, spares him the anxiety of thinking for himself and of having to make responsible decisions in his own behalf. Grumble and complain though he does about his servitude to Hamm, Clov inwardly experiences a sense of relief and comfort in the predictable performance of his familiar, daily tasks. He is never in doubt about what is expected of him, and he is also spared any undue surprises.

Periodically throughout the play, Clov also punctuates the performance of his inspection duties—as well as his tasks in general—with bursts of brief laughter. Beckett himself ascribed true significance to Clov's laughter, its function being one of the manifold "echoes" in the play's carefully insistent repetitions and analogies: he suggested, further, that the quality of Clov's laughter be that of "resigned, reserved bitterness wherever it recurs" (McMillan and Fehsenfeld, 215).

SECTION 2

Section 2 establishes Hamm not only as Clov's master, but also as the play's lordly protagonist. On awakening, Hamm delivers his first soliloquy, beginning with the words "Me—to play" (*EG*, 2), and then addresses his large, blood-stained handkerchief (perhaps evidence of internal hemorrhaging), which he holds spread out before him: "Old stancher!" (*EG*, 2). Removing his dark glasses, Hamm wipes his eyes, face, and glasses with the handkerchief, puts his glasses on again, and then neatly folds and puts the handkerchief in the breast pocket of his dressing gown. Clearing his throat and joining the tips of his fingers, he continues his soliloquy: "Can there be misery—(*he yawns*)—loftier than mine?" (*EG*, 2).

Hamm's soliloquy grows into a slow and lordly litany of his much-endured sufferings before those of the day ahead actually begin. Convinced that the extremity of his suffering is beyond that of others, he is still not convinced it warrants the extremity of a suicide ending. The question becomes, however, For whom is Hamm really performing his soliloquy—Clov, the audience, or himself, the "ham actor" his name implies him to be? His opening "Me—to play" (*EG*, 2) also simultaneously establishes the rhetoric of chess strategy and the rhetoric of playacting as both game and dramatic performance as a continuous, dual metaphor throughout the play.

Summoning Clov by whistle-call, Hamm begins his first dialogue with Clov with an insult, "You pollute the air!" (*EG*, 3), which he immediately follows with an order that Clov get him ready for bed. Just as Clov's opening scene both establishes the *mise-en-scène* (or general stage setting) and begins the play's dialogue with the word *finished,* Hamm's first scene begins the play's action by his expressing the wish to begin his day by going to bed (Cohn 1973, 146).

In his first exchange with Clov, Hamm further develops his self-dramatizing performance, principally to detain Clov and keep him in constant attendance. Behind the bravado with which Hamm holds forth about his eyes (which he claims have turned completely white), his dubious health, and his inquiries about the time of day and the weather conditions outside, however, he is terrified of being left alone, and will do anything to keep Clov in conversation with him or attentive to his physical needs. To Beckett, "There must be maximum aggression between [Hamm and Clov] from [their] first exchange of words onward. Their war is the nucleus of the play" (McMillan and Fehsenfeld, 205).

Like Clov, Hamm needs to make certain each day that nothing has changed in the shelter, including his precarious position as master of the recalcitrant Clov. To reassure himself of his lordly control as well as his ability to maintain some semblance of civilized conversation, Hamm subjects Clov to a series of interrogations such as the following:

> HAMM: Why do you stay with me?
> CLOV: Why do you keep me?
> HAMM: There's no one else.
> CLOV: There's nowhere else.
> (*Pause.*)
> HAMM: You're leaving me all the same.
> CLOV: I'm trying.
> HAMM: You don't love me.
> CLOV: No.
> HAMM: You loved me once.
> CLOV: Once!
> HAMM: I've made you suffer too much.
> (*Pause.*)
> Haven't I?
> CLOV: It's not that.
> HAMM (*shocked*): I haven't made you suffer too much?
> CLOV: Yes!
> HAMM (*relieved*): Ah you gave me a fright!
> (*EG*, 6–7)

At the conclusion of this exchange, Hamm asks Clov if it is time for his painkiller (presumably Hamm's death), which Clov denies. This is the first of six times in the play's action that Hamm asks Clov for his painkiller, which the latter consistently denies.

Later in section 2, when Hamm asks Clov why he does not kill him, Clov replies quite matter-of-factly that it is because he does not know the combination of the cupboard where their food supply is stored. Infuriated, Hamm dismisses Clov to his kitchen, and then vents his contempt on Nagg, his hungry and helpless father ("Accursed progenitor!" *EG*, 9), who has emerged (wearing a nightcap) from one of the ashbins to demand food ("Me pap!" [*EG*, 9]). At Hamm's whistle-call, Clov returns; feeds the toothless Nagg a Spratt's medium dog biscuit, of all things; and then, at Hamm's orders, pushes Nagg back into his bin and closes the lid.

Clov then attempts to quit Hamm's side and return to his kitchen to look, he claims, at its wall. Irate at Clov's daring to leave him helplessly on his own, Hamm demands to know what Clov thinks he sees on his wall, concluding his question with the words "Mene, mene?" Hamm's biblical reference here may be to Daniel 5:26, "MENE; God hath numbered thy kingdom, and finished it." Hamm, who knows the Bible well, may be associating here the disturbing warning written on Belshazzar's wall with his own precarious and uncertain fate in the shelter. Throughout the remainder of section 2, Hamm's efforts to detain Clov in meaningful conversation go as unrewarded as his second request for his painkiller.

For Hamm, acting—or self-dramatization—has become an essential means of survival. It has also become a highly developed stratagem for maintaining personal sanity as well as control in what would otherwise be intolerable and unbearable circumstances. Though Hamm may never have actually appeared on stage in his life, he can, nevertheless, be appropriately described, in the current parlance of the entertainment world, as an "actor type." In keeping with the actor type, he thrives, by nature, on performance in every aspect of his daily life, automatically transforming incidents and events happening around him into scenarios for his own egocentric displays of rhetorical and emotional exhibitionism. From Hamm's point of view, what really matters to him or what actually happens to the rest of the world is significant only insofar as it affects him personally. Hamm, for example, often gives the impression that he holds strong opinions on a wide variety of subjects, but on closer inspection, his opinions are often less important to him as a basis for his code of behavior than as opportunities for impressing others—especially the recalcitrant Clov—with a dazzling display of rhetoric or vituperation. Though Hamm, in his first monologue, presents himself as a well-defined and self-assured character, his concerted efforts to maintain a constant blustering bravado throughout the remainder of the play's action belie this initial impression, which eventually disintegrates, little by little, into a variety of poses, prejudices, opinions, and emotional attitudes that do not reveal, despite their vehemence, the presence of a coherent personality behind them.

Critic Michael Anderson, in his study of John Arden, John Osborne, and Harold Pinter, entitled *Anger and Detachment* (1976), offers a cogent description of the actor type, which Hamm exemplifies both in personality and in self-dramatizing behavior. To Anderson, the actor type is "a kind of exposed essence of human being [who when] on stage . . . steps into one role after another, and [hence] must be on intimate terms with the entire range of human emotions."[7] Anderson contends, however, that "when [the actor type] takes off the greasepaint he lacks the protective personality that most of us carry around to shield our true nature from the prying eyes of the world; [as a result,] the need to display and communicate passion which is his stock in trade is not something that can be left behind in the dressing-room along with the wigs and the make-up" (Anderson, 22). Further, Anderson contends, the actor type is "always in search of an audience: all in all he can prove an enthralling but wholly demanding companion, supremely arrogant and yet supremely vulnerable" (Anderson, 22).

Perhaps what may account for much of the protagonistic appeal an actor type such as Hamm may have for us, whether as audience or readers, is that, as Anderson suggests, "we are all of us secretly convinced that we are the centre of the universe, and that we have been given the major role in a gigantic drama in which no-one else, even among those tied to us by the closest links of friendship, family or love, shares our star billing" (Anderson, 22). But unlike Hamm, "most of us have learnt from hard experience that even if we play the star role in a drama of our own, we are mostly walk-ons in other people's scenarios, and we tend to keep our egos on a fairly tight lead accordingly" (Anderson, 22).

Anderson also suggests, that the pleasure we often experience in getting to know actor types such as Hamm, whether on- or offstage, may result, in part, from their ability to draw "us into a charmed circle where . . . we are listeners, watchers and sharers rather than part of the great outside world which feeds the actor type[s] with [their] material. We are, in short, an audience, and the bond of emotional identification which exists between the actor[s] and [their] audience is cemented by the complicity that links the actor type[s] to a psychological hunger lurking within all of us" (Anderson, 22).

Section 3

Section 3 introduces Nagg and Nell (the latter wearing a lace cap), the two elderly occupants of the two ashbins on stage, thus establishing the play's entire cast of four characters. In their extensive scene together, perhaps one of the most poignant love scenes in postwar drama, they strive for romantic intimacy by use of the only means their aging physical deterioration has left them: words.

> NELL: What is it, my pet?
> (*Pause.*)
> Time for love?
> NAGG: Were you asleep?
> NELL: Oh, no!
> NAGG: Kiss me.
> NELL: We can't.
> NAGG: Try.
> (*Their heads strain towards each other, fail to meet, fall apart again.*)
> NELL: Why this farce, day after day? (*EG*, 14)

When not complaining about their losses of sight, hearing, and teeth, they impotently vent their rage against Hamm for the humiliation of his not having Clov provide them with adequate food and a regular change of sawdust (rather than mere sand from the nearby seashore) in their ashbins. At other times, they attempt to distract themselves from their distress by telling jokes, such as Nagg's ribald retelling of an old Jewish story of the tailor who took more than three months to make a decent pair of trousers, the results of which proved more satisfactory than God's six-day effort to create the world. Or they—especially Nell—try being romantically reminiscent about events and details of their youth:

> NELL: Can you believe it?
> NAGG: What?
> NELL: That we once went out rowing on Lake Como.
> (*Pause.*)
> One April afternoon.
> NAGG: We had got engaged the day before.
> NELL: Engaged!
> NAGG: You were in such fits that we capsized. By rights we should have been drowned.
> NELL: It was because I felt happy.
> NAGG (*indignant*): It was not, it was not, it was my story and nothing else! Happy! Don't you laugh at it still? Every time I tell it. Happy! (*EG*, 21)

Wearied by Nagg and Nell, Hamm interrupts their romantic reminiscences to announce that he is experiencing something rather like a heart that is throbbing or dripping in his head (possibly a parasympathetic response to Clov's preoccupation with an "impossible heap" of grain that grows, grain by grain, imperceptibly larger each day). When Nagg chuckles cautiously at Hamm's distress, Nell overtly admonishes him, but then concedes, in a lowered voice, that nothing is truly funnier than unhappiness.

But why are Hamm and Clov's faces very red and Nagg and Nell's very white? When questioned on this point, Beckett often replied that the faces of the four characters are boldly colored so as to provide dramatic contrast, such as that which exists between opposing pieces in a chess game. Some scholars, finding this explanation neither sufficient nor satisfying, have created their own inspired theories, such as that of critic David H. Helsa. According to Helsa, Nagg and Nell's faces are white as well as cold as ice, not simply because they may represent chess pieces, but because they may at one time have formed a very active energy system that is now dead, or nearly so. According to Helsa, "As befits energy systems which are younger, [Hamm and Clov's faces] are 'very red.' They are still active, each after his fashion; though it is clear that the metaphor of the chess game here takes precedence over the metaphor drawn from thermodynamics, else their faces would be described rather as a fading pink in token of the subsidence of their late strengths."[8]

Section 3 concludes with Hamm's demanding silence of Nagg and Nell, and then pleading for an end to his own torment, "Will this never finish?" (*EG,* 23), thus echoing the urgent concern for "finishing" matters that Clov expresses in his opening soliloquy in section 1. In compliance with Hamm's demand, Nagg disappears into his ashbin, closing the lid behind him, but Nell does not move. Both furious and exasperated, Hamm shouts in a Richard III frenzy, "My kingdom for a nightman!" (*EG,* 23), then summons Clov with a loud whistle-call to rid him of the offending Nagg and Nell.

Thus, sections 1–3 provide the requisites of a conventional play's beginning: exposition of situation, characters, and action. Ultimately, they will be symmetrically balanced by the last three sections' (14–16) conclusion (McMillan and Fehsenfeld, 188).

Section 4

Section 4 presents an extended dialogue between Hamm and Clov in which the former goes out of his way to be as difficult and demanding as possible to demonstrate that he is still the lordly master of the situation. Overhearing Nell, for example, urge Clov to leave him and go away into the desert, Hamm angrily orders Clov to "bottle" Nagg and Nell in their respective ashbins and screw down the lids. Then, when Clov refuses for the third time in the play's action to give him his painkiller, Hamm commands Clov to take him for a little turn around the room in his armchair, ending with Hamm being positioned in the exact center of the room. Further, Hamm insists that Clov "hug the walls" as much as possible when pushing Hamm's chair so as to ensure a fuller turn (and tour) of the room: presumably Hamm's kingdom or domain. Clov obeys (but purposefully not to Hamm's precise specifications) and then resumes his obedient, attendant position beside the armchair, muttering, "If I could kill him [Hamm] I'd die happy" (*EG*, 27).

As section 4 defines the existence of Hamm, Clov, Nagg, and Nell *inside* the shelter, section 5, which follows immediately, defines life *outside* the shelter as Clov ascertains it during his "second inspection," this time with a telescope (McMillan and Fehsenfeld, 188).

In section 4, as well as in the play overall, Beckett places considerably more dramatic emphasis on the blind and paralyzed Hamm than on his crippled servant, Clov. But Clov's vital presence as a volitional character with whom Hamm must continually reckon is essential to the play's central dynamic. In *Endgame*, critic Charles R. Lyons perceptively notes, Beckett presents a protagonist who performs a number of exercises that enact his interpretations of the role or roles that collectively constitute his identity. In that sense, Lyons suggests, Hamm's behavior can be viewed as an existential performance that depends heavily on Clov's presence to stimulate Hamm to imagine himself as the object of Clov's perception. Further, Lyons suggests, "while that perception confirms [Hamm's] sense of his own existence, it remains equivocal on at least two bases: first of all, Clov is always an alien figure and, secondly, Clov perceives a performance rather than real behaviour. Hamm creates an image of himself for Clov—and thus for himself. Hamm's being is equivocal to [Clov] for whom he performs, to himself, and to the audience."[9]

SECTION 5

Section 5 is almost dominated by Clov's vaudeville antics with the ladder and telescope. When Hamm tells him to observe the weather conditions outside the shelter by sighting with his telescope first through the earth window and then through the sea window, Clov starts an extended comic routine of confusion: which to fetch first, the telescope or the ladder? His Chaplinesque antics, rather than livening things up, fail to arouse even a faint laugh from Hamm. When finally, exasperated by Clov's delaying tactics, Hamm demands the weather report, his worst suspicions are confirmed. Outside both windows, everything is "corpsed" (*EG,* 30), the light is sunk, nothing exists on the horizon, the waves are lead, the sun is zero, and all is gray.

During these ladder-and-telescope vaudeville antics, Ruby Cohn suggests, "Hamm and Clov make contradictory comments on the play as play. HAMM: 'This is deadly.' But CLOV: 'Things are livening up.' It is in the middle of this comic scene that Clov invents the word 'Corpsed'" (Cohn 1973, 148).

By getting Clov to observe carefully the horrifying world outside the shelter, Hamm may, in part, be trying to get him to realize the actual conditions he will have to face should he ever carry out his threats to desert Hamm. This motive notwithstanding, Hamm is personally disturbed by Clov's report that everything outside the shelter is "corpsed."

Critic Michael Robinson, in his Beckett study entitled *The Long Sonata of the Dead* (1969), suggests that in section 5, Hamm may, in fact, be using Clov as a pretext to describe his own doubtful condition: "This is the agony of the man who is condemned to wait on the ledge before Paradise throughout eternity. Unlike [Dante's] Belacqua in the shadow of his rock, who could see the heavens revolving with a purpose and therefore was content to dream in the secure knowledge of a prescribed end to his exile from God, Hamm cannot anticipate his release from time. In his world the moments move so slowly that astral time, the sun, moon, stars, seasons, are all compounded in the same, general colourlessness."[10] Also, Robinson suggests, "If life is as it appears to Hamm then its existence is intolerable and ought not to be permitted. Hamm, more extreme than Ivan Karamazov, returns the ticket of life, not the ticket to heaven. He has no pity for suffering humanity or rather his pity, like his compassion, is taken to a logical extreme where the individual has no place and the conclusion is extinction" (Robinson, 276).

SECTION 6

Section 6 centers on Hamm's interrogation of Clov concerning any possible signs of life on earth, culminating in the burlesque flea scene:

> HAMM: What's happening?
> CLOV: Something is taking its course.
> (*Pause.*)
> HAMM: Clov!
> CLOV (*impatiently*): What is it?
> HAMM: We're not beginning to . . . to . . . mean something?
> CLOV: Mean something! You and I, mean something!
> (*Brief laugh.*)
> Ah that's a good one!
> HAMM: I wonder.
> (*Pause.*)
> Imagine if a rational being came back to earth, wouldn't he be
> liable to get ideas into his head if he observed us long enough.
> (*EG*, 32–33)

To divert Hamm or perhaps to change the topic of their disturbing conversation, Clov announces that he has found a flea in his trousers. This sign of life right within the shelter deeply perturbs Hamm ("But humanity might start from there all over again! Catch him, for the love of God!" [*EG*, 33]). Fetching some insecticide, Clov "loosens the top of his trousers, pulls it forward, and shakes a generous amount of powder into the aperture. He [then] stoops, looks, waits, starts, frenziedly shakes more powder, [and then once again] stoops, looks, and waits" (*EG*, 34).

Hamm wants definite assurance that Clov has succeeded in destroying this possible alternate form of life in their "midst" that

40

might survive him and renew the evolutionary line to mankind (McMillan and Fehsenfeld, 188):

> HAMM: Did you get him?
> CLOV: Looks like it.
> (*He drops the tin and adjusts his trousers.*)
> Unless he's laying doggo.
> HAMM: Laying! Lying you mean. Unless he's lying doggo. . . .
> Use your head, can't you. If he was laying we'd be bitched.
> (*EG*, 34)

Characters and situations having been defined in sections 1–5, now *Endgame* progresses to the statement of its major themes. Sections 6 and 7 present the question to be resolved in this play: the possibility of endings, and the likelihood of unexpected new beginnings. The action with the flea of section 6 symbolizes beginnings threatened by scratchings. Clov's Chaplinesque burlesque of flea-powdering implies that the flea might yet be the ultimate source of renewed life on earth that must be destroyed at all costs if a true ending to mankind is to be definitely achieved.

Clov's burlesque of flea-powdering in section 6, as well as his vaudeville antics with the stepladder and the telescope in section 5 and throughout much of the play, suggests that Beckett's sense of stage comedy may have been significantly influenced by both the Dublin music halls and the great Hollywood silent-film comedies that were all a part of Beckett's youth. Hamm and Clov's stichomythic dialogue exchanges in *Endgame,* like those of Vladimir and Estragon in *Godot,* demonstrate strong affinities with the comic cross-talk acts of the music hall. Moreover, Beckett was also a great admirer of the silent films of Charles Chaplin (1889–1977), Buster Keaton (1895–1966), Harold Lloyd (1893–1971), and Harry Langdon (1884–1944), which, according to actor Jack MacGowran, "provided a strong influence on Beckett's own mature writing, particularly the vaudevillian kind of touches one sees here and there in his work" (Gontarski, 222).

Chaplin, who holds the distinction of being the one actor most often portrayed on screen by other actors, was a superb mime who brought pathos and compassion to his films that few of his contemporaries could match. His little tramp figure with little bowler, too-small jacket and too-large pants held up with string, enormous boots on turned-out feet, mustache, and cane, remains one of the screen's most enduring images. Keaton, known affectionately as "The Great Stone Face," was rivaled only by Chaplin in his mastery of screen comedy. The distinction of his comic style was his ability to perform seemingly impossible acrobatic gags and to maintain his own "stone face" personality. In his almost impersonal characterization and in the subtlety and grace of his physical humor, Keaton was incomparable as an actor and a director. The bespectacled Lloyd, though not possessing the subtlety of Chaplin and Keaton, was equally popular at the box office for his skill at performing acrobatic tricks, usually on top of high buildings. The sad-faced Langdon, also a contemporary of Chaplin and Keaton, began his film career by appearing in many Mack Sennett Keystone shorts. His creation of a comic persona projecting a mixture of Pierrot and middle-aged baby has been considerably underrated.

The comic influence of these silent-film actors notwithstanding, Beckett did not necessarily see himself as a comic writer, for, according to Jack MacGowran, "the humor in [Beckett's] plays, for the most part, is one of ironic laughter. . . . Beckett has the ability to write one line that contains tragedy and laughter at the same time" (Gontarski, 222). When MacGowran was once asked to elaborate further on his often-quoted perception that Beckett is an optimistic playwright, he responded, "Yes, but he's not entirely optimistic. There are the moments of pessimism and doubt, which I think are normal to us all. Otherwise, he's as optimistic a writer as any you'll find" (Gontarski, 222).

To MacGowran, Beckett is actually a highly realistic playwright: "[Beckett] talks of the human condition as it is, and sometimes it's not very pleasant in the world today. He's got no rose-colored glasses; he dispensed with them long ago. He sees life as it really is and has tremendous compassion for humankind. Man's inhumanity to man upsets him gravely" (Gontarski, 222). Further, to MacGowran, Beckett is the greatest realist writer of this generation: "He's an extreme realist. Pinter has said openly in the press, 'Beckett to me is the acme of all the great writers of this generation. Without Beckett, I would not be writing. He rubs my nose in the shit and the more he rubs it in it, the more I like him.' And this, I think, is a great compliment from one very good playwright to another" (Gontarski, 222).

SECTION 7

Section 7 begins with Hamm and Clov in dialogue concerning their dubious chances for escape (by raft to the south in possibly shark-infested waters) from their present hopeless situation. Interrupting their discourse of alternating scornful reproaches, Hamm asks for the fourth time in the play's action for his painkiller, which Clov adamantly refuses to give him. Hamm then shifts to the tactic of reminding Clov "with prophetic relish" (*EG*, 36) of his own impending "slow and solitary dying, which may be [Hamm's] image of his own" (Cohn 1973, 148):

> HAMM: One day you'll be blind, like me. You'll be sitting there, a speck in the void, in the dark, for ever, like me. . . . Yes, one day you'll know what it is, you'll be like me, except that you won't have had pity on anyone and because there won't be anyone left to pity you. (*EG*, 36)

By speculating on such a terrible curse, Hamm hopes to discourage any possibility of Clov's leaving him, Nagg, and Nell. He further reminds Clov that it was he who took Clov in as a child and took care of him like a father. Notwithstanding, Clov threatens, for the seventh time, to leave Hamm. Believing he still has the upper hand in the situation, Hamm asks Clov to fetch him the toy the latter has been making for him: a black dog with only three legs. Unfinished though the toy is, it is already a cripple, like Clov. Hamm asks Clov to stand it on its precarious three feet, facing him. Holding the dog in a standing position, Clov guides Hamm's hand toward its head. Feeling in control of the situation once again, Hamm is satisfied ("Leave him like that, standing there imploring me [for a walk or a bone]" [*EG,* 41]). When Clov releases his hold on the toy dog, however, it falls on its side, and the blind Hamm does not know it.

Section 7 presents in Hamm's dog the unfinished toy made by servant for master, and intended for the time when all Hamm's human company has gone. Further, Ruby Cohn suggests, the "imploring [toy] dog mirrors the imploring man of Hamm's chronicle, which mirrors Nagg and Clov imploring Hamm on stage" (Cohn 1973, 148). Dominated by taunting discussion of what "goes on in the end," the section contains the play's first prophecy of end, and in its "implicit allusion to the parasitical relationship of fleas and dogs [, it also] underscores [Hamm's obsession with bringing matters to a definite end, which is being thwarted] by undesired new beginnings [of life]" (McMillan and Fehsenfeld, 188).

SECTION 8

Section 8 further develops Clov's growing servant-master/son-father rebellion against Hamm. Its references range from Hamm's inquiry about Mother Pegg, another struggling survivor, who lives nearby, to his own story of the mad painter, and Clov's idea of using the alarm clock to signal his final departure.

Hamm begins this section by wondering about the welfare of Mother Pegg. When Clov reports that both Mother Pegg and her light are extinguished and he has no intention of burying her, Hamm replies as follows:

> HAMM: She was bonny once, like a flower of the field.
> (*With reminiscent leer.*)
> And a great one for the men!
> CLOV: We too were bonny—once. It's a rare thing not to have been bonny—once. (*EG,* 42)

Hamm then demands his gaff, but despite his struggling efforts, is unable to move in his armchair without Clov's assistance. He recounts the story of the mad painter (or possibly engraver) who, believing the end of the world had come, had been confined to an insane asylum. Fond of the man, Hamm would visit him, take him by the hand, and drag him to the window to assure him that the world outside was indeed teeming with life. Invariably, however, the artist would snatch away his hand and retreat to his corner, because "all he had seen was ashes" (*EG*, 44). Beckett's direction of the 1967 Berlin production of *Endspiel* left no doubt that the mad painter retreating from the sight of the ashes outdoors is analogous to Clov, who, earlier in the play's action, has described nature as a waste and expressed a preference to stare instead at the wall in his kitchen, with its "nice dimensions, nice proportions" (*EG*, 2; McMillan and Fehsenfeld, 222). Beckett's 1967 stage direction notwithstanding, the story of the mad painter may also have considerable personal significance for Hamm as well. Given the animated and engrossed manner in which Hamm tells the story, he may be identifying with the painter, whose horrifying world vision is similar to his own present one. But unlike the painter, whose vision is illusory, Hamm is convinced that what he sees is real and anything but illusory.

In despair, Hamm questions whether "this thing" (presumably their hopeless and meaningless existence) "has gone on long enough" (*EG*, 45). Clov agrees with him that it has, and though Hamm cannot leave Clov, Clov can indeed leave Hamm. When Hamm requests a good-bye kiss, Clov refuses him. Hamm then asks how he will know whether Clov has left or died in his kitchen, since the stench of his rotting corpse would be indistinguishable from the general stench of corpses around him. Clov's solution is to set the alarm clock as indicative signal: if it rings, he has gone; if it does not, he is dead. To rehearse, the two men set the alarm bell of the clock, reacting to its ringing like two music buffs devoted to the movements of a symphony (CLOV: "The end is terrific!—HAMM: "I prefer the middle" [*EG*, 488]). In *Endgame,* Ruby Cohn notes, "clocks do not tell time but sound an alarm" (Cohn 1973, 149).

Section 8 ends with Hamm asking for the fifth time for his painkiller, which Clov once again emphatically denies. Hamm then wants to tell another story, but Clov refuses to listen. Hamm then has

Clov wake up Nagg and promises the latter a sugarplum if he will be an attentive listener while Hamm tells his story. Nagg complies. Section 8 thus "concludes the expository portion of the play with a summary recapitulation. It is based upon the scene referring to Mother Pegg, Hamm's attempt to move himself about with the [gaff], the account of the mad painter who recoiled from what he saw outside, and the [alarm clock] which will signal that Clov has departed and will not answer Hamm's [whistle-call]" (McMillan and Fehsenfeld, 188). Further, "In a world where there is real need expressed in appeals for aid, self-help is not sufficient, retreat into a corner at the prospect of a world in ashes is equally insufficient, and those who might respond to appeals will ultimately be absent" (McMillan and Fehsenfeld, 188–89).

SECTION 9

Section 9 centers on Hamm's first lengthy monologue, his reminiscence of a poor man (presumably a beggar) and his baby who on Christmas Eve had once sought Hamm's charity. The technical beginning of the play now over, and its exposition completed, its next focus pertains to the plot. Hamm's vivid description of the baby son's total dependence on a parent seems to be a deliberately allegorical reminder to Nagg and Nell, as well as Clov, of their total dependence on his bounty. Hamm recounts in the story his eventual consent to take the man into his service, to provide "bread for his brat" (*EG*, 52), and to give shelter to the baby and parent. Enthroned in his armchair, old Hamm now tells the story with relish, thoroughly enjoying his recollection of tyrannical power and cruel authority. In his histrionic delivery of it, he resorts to every gimmick and device he can find in his ham actor's bag of tricks. Further, Ruby Cohn notes, "Hamm limits his critical comments to esthetics, which give all the harder edge to the poignant situation in the story" (Cohn 1973, 149). To critics Dougald McMillan and Martha Fehsenfeld, "This first instalment of [Hamm's] story stands apart in the middle dividing the play between its comic first half essentially concentrated upon exposition, and its more tragic last half essentially concentrated upon concluding action. The narrative element begun here, although a subplot of the possibility of Hamm's harboring another child, is continued later and then concluded at the end of the play" (McMillan and Fehsenfeld, 189). Moreover, McMillan and Fehsenfeld note, "In this first presentation the story may still be seen as part of a comic beginning and there is still laughter, albeit sardonic, at the mention of the child. In the final section the laughter will be replaced by concentration on the tragic fate of 'hunger, cold, and death to crown it all' which awaits the child" (McMillan and Fehsenfeld, 189). Jack MacGowran, who played Clov in several productions of *Endgame,* recalls performing this scene as if Clov were "the person who was brought there by the [beggar-father], so that the story is not really fiction at all. It's a retelling of those early years, which Clov may or may not remember because he has been there so long" (Gontarski, 219).

SECTION 10

Section 10 reveals via both Hamm's prayer to God for salvation and Nagg's curse on him ("Yes, I hope I'll live till then, to hear you calling me like when you were a tiny boy, and were frightened, in the dark, and I was your only hope" [*EG,* 56]), the desperate, lonely fate that awaits Hamm, the play's protagonist. Both his pleas to God and to humanity will be unanswered (McMillan and Fehsenfeld, 189). Moreover, Nagg's curse is, to Beckett, one of the major climactic points in the play, and Nagg's delivery of his speech of paternal spite, his *malediction* (McMillan and Fehsenfeld, 183), must be done with all the venom possible to muster.

In section 10, Hamm also orders Clov as well as Nagg and Nell to pray to God, and as critic Michael Robinson notes, "although the image of a group of derelicts pantomiming a spiritual action is both ludicrous and amusing, Hamm's cry 'The bastard! He doesn't exist!' contains more agony than pathos" (Robinson, 27). Robinson also notes that "Although the prayer is made without any expectations of a reply, the pain of [God's] absence is still very real for it is followed by a greater silence, loneliness and despair. The questions of Ivan Karamazov still echo faintly behind all the writings, the silences and the waitings: can I forgive God for not existing, and if He did exist, could I forgive Him for all the suffering He has caused?" (Robinson, 27).

Section 10 concludes with Nagg's curse on Hamm, and thus echoes Hamm's curse-prophecy in section 7 regarding Clov's ultimate fate—"that he will end in solitude" (Cohn 1973, 149). Further, given Hamm's dramatic dominance throughout section 10, it is scarcely noticeable in the action that Nagg, failing to get Nell to answer or respond to his desperate knocks on her ashbin lid, sinks back disconsolately into his ashbin, closing its lid behind him (Cohn 1973, 149).

SECTION 11

According to Beckett, the basis, the dark foundation, of *Endgame* is despair, and Hamm sets its zero point (McMillan and Fehsenfeld, 221) by opening section 11 with a line from the close of the masque scene in *The Tempest*: "Our revels now are ended" (4.1.148). This ironic evocation of Prospero clearly announces a change from comic to tragic mode, and the approach of the end. The action that follows in the second half of *Endgame* is a mere passing of time to delay the inevitable end. According to Ruby Cohn, at this point in the play's action, the Vladimir-Estragon (*Waiting for Godot*) aspect of *Endgame* is finished: "repartee, memories, story, prayer. Hamm has exhausted his ingenuity in killing time. He will dissolve his royal role into that of pawn" (Cohn 1973, 149). In addition, critics Dougald McMillan and Martha Fehsenfeld suggest that "Clov's 'dream of order' and his unsuccessful attempt to pick up and dispose properly of all the stage properties, Hamm's 'news' that his story is progressing, and the possible death of Nell are all signs of the end.

Also, the play within the play of Hamm and Clov brings a liberating change of atmosphere from tense drama to relaxed cheerfulness" (McMillan and Fehsenfeld, 189).

When Hamm sends Clov to check whether or not Nell is dead, Clov replies, "Looks like it" (*EG*, 62), and Hamm raises his toque (presumably in respect for the dead) for the second time in the play's action; in section 8, Hamm raises his toque for the first time as a benedictory gesture in response to Clov's "God be with the days!" (*EG*, 44). Beckett, when once asked if Nell does indeed die during section 11, "entrenched himself smilingly behind an ironic disclaimer of special knowledge— 'So it seems, but no one knows'" (McMillan and Fehsenfeld, 213). If Nell actually dies, Ruby Cohn contends, then "something new is possible in [*Endgame*'s] stage world, but her death is never verified. Asked about Nagg, Clov replies: 'He's crying,' and Hamm retorts with the most mordantly spurious logic of the play: 'Then he's living'" (Cohn 1973, 150).

SECTION 12

Section 12, which depicts Hamm's "second turn" about the room in his armchair pushed by Clov, presents the "former world in a new state of quiescence. There is no light from the earth window and the sea is calm. This [information] is met by Hamm with an attitude of tragic acceptance" (McMillan and Fehsenfeld, 189). At the completion of this "second turn," Clov returns Hamm in his armchair to his former place of position in the room, and remains standing, with his head bowed, behind Hamm's chair. Hamm then calls twice for his father (presumably out of some desperate, vestigial need for paternal comfort and reassurance), but when he receives no answer, sends Clov to find out whether Nagg has heard either of his two calls. Clov reports that Nagg (who is no longer crying but instead is sucking a biscuit) has heard only one call from Hamm, but is not certain whether it was Hamm's first or second call that he heard.

SECTION 13

Section 13 consists of resumed dialogue between Hamm and
Clov concerning the actual status of their tenuous master-servant/
father-son relationship. Unable or unwilling to provide Hamm with a
lap rug to protect him against the chill, Clov also refuses to show any
expression of affection:

> HAMM: Kiss me.
> (*Pause.*)
> Will you not kiss me?
> CLOV: No.
> HAMM: On the forehead.
> CLOV: I won't kiss you anywhere.
> HAMM (*holding out his hand*): Give me your hand at least.
> (*Pause.*)
> Will you not give me your hand?
> CLOV: I won't touch you. (*EG,* 67)

It has been suggested that "Clov's inability to provide a rug to keep
Hamm warm and his unloving refusal to touch Hamm are foreshad-
owing and preparation for Clov's ultimate refusal to respond to
Hamm's call with which the play culminates" (McMillan and
Fehsenfeld, 189–90). Section 13 concludes with Hamm asking
for his toy dog (presumably as a substitute for the companionship
Clov refuses him), but then changing his mind. Clov then retires
to his kitchen to kill the rat he says he has discovered there before
it dies.

SECTION 14

Section 14 presents Hamm's penultimate monologue: his "role,"
which he begins in a state of calm reflection and builds, in progressive
stages, to states of pleading, rage, and then pure meditation (McMillan
and Fehsenfeld, 227). In this monologue, Hamm expresses feelings of

guilt as well as "the anticipation, in [his] imagination, of what happens after the end of the play" (McMillan and Fehsenfeld, 227).

> HAMM: It will be the end and there I'll be, wondering what can
> have brought it on and wondering what can have . . .
> (*he hesitates*)
> . . . why it was so long coming.
> (*Pause.*)
> There I'll be, in the old shelter, alone against the silence and . . .
> (*he hesitates*)
> . . . the stillness. If I can hold my peace, and sit quiet, it will be all
> over with sound, and motion, all over and done with. (*EG,* 69)

In his 1967 staging of *Endspiel* in Berlin, Beckett suggested to Ernst Schroeder, who played Hamm, that he perform this particular monologue with actions that would appropriately anticipate those of the last scene of the play—with, for example, Hamm assuming a still, upright sitting position, with his arms resting motionless on those of the armchair.

Sections 14–16 of *Endgame* provide a concentrated theatrical conclusion to the play, focusing on Hamm's "last soliloquy" in sections 14 and 16, which Clov interrupts with further action in section 15. As in those earlier sections of the play which develop its themes, no absolute finality is actually achieved (McMillan and Fehsenfeld, 190).

SECTION 15

Section 15 presents Clov's emancipation from Hamm, as well as the play's ultimate and fatal question: What, if anything, has actually happened? It also delays Hamm's self-prophecy of final isolation as indicated in the preceding section by introducing new beginnings and completions that alternate in a regular pattern (McMillan and Fehsenfeld, 190). The rat in the kitchen, for example, has escaped, so that the possibility of life continuing to evolve is maintained. Also, the time for Hamm's painkiller has finally arrived, but his supply has been depleted. Further, Clov's "third inspection" of the conditions outside the shelter reveals the fact-or-fantasy existence of a young boy who might possibly reestablish a relationship like the one Hamm has with Clov, which seems now to be ending. And finally, Hamm and Clov engage in their "mutual dismissal," verbally, at least, ending their relationship (McMillan and Fehsenfeld, 190).

In section 15, Ruby Cohn notes that "The mutual Hamm-Clov recriminations explode into violence, when Clov hits Hamm on the head with the toy-dog. Hamm pleads that Clov use an axe or a gaff, those deadly weapons of tragedy" (Cohn 1973, 150). Cohn also notes that "When Clov announces that there are no more coffins, Hamm retorts with the last sadistic piece of spurious logic: 'Then let it end!' But the small boy—[a potential procreator]—precludes an end. Hamm frees Clov, who . . . [u]nlike Hamm, . . . is not a hamm-actor; [Clov] assumes no role . . . [and] knows [only] pain. At the last Hamm and Clov address each other with courteous formality—for the first and only time in the play" (Cohn 1973, 150).

Further, section 15 includes what Beckett once described as Clov's monologue of the "five dispensers of life's consolations[: friendship, beauty, wisdom, mercy, and love]" (McMillan and Fehsenfeld, 226). It poses an extreme challenge for the actor playing Clov, for he must deliver it tonelessly and work with so few means:

> CLOV: I say to myself—sometimes. Clov, you must learn to suffer better than that if you want them to weary of punishing you—one day. I say to myself—sometimes, Clov, you must be there better than that if you want them to let you go—one day. But I feel too old, and too far, to form new habits. Good, it'll never end, I'll never go.
> (*Pause.*)
> Then one day, suddenly it ends, it changes, I don't understand, it dies, or it's me, I don't understand, that either. I ask the words that remain—sleeping, waking, morning, evening. They have nothing to say.
> (*Pause.*)
> I open the door of the cell and go. I am so bowed I only see my feet, if I open my eyes, and between my legs a little trail of black

dust. I say to myself that the earth is extinguished, though I never
saw it lit.
(*Pause.*)
It's easy going.
(*Pause.*)
When I fall I'll weep for happiness.
(*Pause. He goes towards door.*) (*EG,* 80–81)

Clov is realizing here that he must learn to suffer, and he must learn to
do it better, because, as Beckett once stated, "when one has given the
tyrant [Hamm] his full account of suffering, he lets his victim go. Only
when one has given life its full share can one leave it" (McMillan and
Fehsenfeld, 226).

No analysis of section 15, as well as section 8, of *Endgame,* however, would be complete without some attention to Hamm and Clov's
significant remarks about old Mother Pegg and her request of Hamm
for oil for her lamp. In section 15, when Hamm and Clov debate the
wasted state of the world outside the shelter, Hamm protests that he
does not understand or really care about what has happened. Clov
challenges Hamm's pose of feigned ignorance by reminding him of his
cruel mistreatment of Mother Pegg and his harsh refusal of her request
for oil for her empty lamp. Clov is convinced that without oil for her
lamp, Mother Pegg must surely have died of the fatal outer darkness.
This exchange between Hamm and Clov, critic Kristin Morrison suggests, "contains clear reference to the New Testament parable about
the wise and foolish virgins, a story about salvation and damnation,
ultimate life and death"[11]:

> Then shall the kingdom of heaven be likened unto ten virgins,
> which took their lamps, and went forth to meet the bridegroom.
> And five of them were wise, and five were foolish. They that were
> foolish took their lamps, and took no oil with them: but the wise
> took oil in their vessels with their lamps. While the bridegroom
> tarried, they all slumbered and slept. And at midnight there was a
> cry made, Behold the bridegroom cometh; go ye out to meet him.
> Then all those virgins arose, and trimmed their lamps. And the
> foolish said unto the wise, Give us of your oil; for our lamps are

gone out. But the wise answered, saying, Not so; lest there be not enough for us and you: but go ye rather to them that sell, and buy for yourselves. And while they went to buy, the bridegroom came; and they that were ready went in with him to the marriage: and the door was shut. Afterward came also the other virgins, saying, Lord. Lord, open to us. But he answered and said, Verily I say unto you, I know you not. Watch therefore; for ye know neither the day nor the hour wherein the Son of man cometh. (Matthew 25:1–13)

Also, according to Morrison, Matthew 22 contains an allied parable, also about a marriage feast, that develops this imagery further, ending with a description of the damnation of one who is not properly prepared: "Then said the king to the servants, Bind him hand and foot, and take him away, and cast him into outer darkness; there shall be weeping and gnashing of teeth. For many are called, but few are chosen" (Matthew 22:1–14). The words *oil, lamp, hell,* and *darkness* in Beckett's passage, Morrison suggests, trigger these biblical allusions to the New Testament. Morrison also suggests the following:

> Kingdom of heaven, wedding feast, light in the darkness, the savior who comes unexpectedly: these are the words of hope and promise, the encouragement and the warning the parables contain. They express in little the whole Christian message of salvation, here used for ironic contrast, to intensify the sense of hopelessness in *Endgame.* Hamm is the god who damns by withholding, or by being unable to provide, the means that make life possible, whether it be bread in the wilderness (which he had earlier denied to the multitudes) or light in the darkness (which the lamp and the oil represent). (Morrison, 94)

Further, Morrison contends, Mother Pegg's name may be intentionally used by Beckett to suggest crucifixion, though that particular allusion seems much less germane to the details of *Endgame* than the set of parables she cites from the Book of Matthew. To Morrison, "*Endgame* is rich in specific references to food, to bread, to inner place and outer wilderness, to light and darkness, to salvation and loss—to what are the central images of these particular parables. The allusion itself does not change or add anything to the sense of misery and hopelessness that the play has previously established; it simply intensifies what is already there" (Morrison, 94–95). Further, Morrison suggests, "The biblical allusion lurking in this particular passage universalizes it by quietly reminding the audience [and readers] of the words they have heard before" (Morrison, 95).

SECTION 16

Section 16 concludes the play with Hamm's final monologue, beginning with the words "Old endgame lost of old, play and lose and have done with losing" (*EG*, 82). Before he launches full force into it, however, Hamm throws away his gaff, raises his toque for a third and final time (presumably in acknowledgment of his own impending death), and pronounces the profane blessing "Peace to our . . . arses" (*EG*, 82).

During all this, Clov enters, dressed inappropriately for the road in a Panama hat, tweed coat, raincoat over his arm, umbrella, and bag, and halts by the door, his eyes riveted on Hamm until the end of the latter's final monologue. In his impractical and clumsy travel gear, Clov is a comic portrait of a person who has never "gotten away" and seems completely incapable of ever doing so (McMillan and Fehsenfeld, 235).

After his monologue, Hamm calls out twice for his father. When there is no answer, he throws away his toy dog and his whistle, calling out for Clov, who does not answer, either.

> HAMM: No? Good.
> (*He takes out the [blood-stained] handkerchief.*)
> Since that's the way we're playing it . . .
> (*he unfolds handkerchief*)
> . . . let's play it that way . . .
> (*he unfolds*)
> . . . and speak no more about it . . .
> (*he finishes unfolding*)

... speak no more.
(*He holds handkerchief spread out before him.*)
Old stancher!
(*Pause.*)
You ... remain.
(*Pause. He covers his face with handkerchief, lowers his arms to armrests, remaining motionless.*)
(*Brief tableau.*) (*EG,* 84)

According to Beckett, Hamm covers his face with the blood-stained handkerchief, not to signify death, but "only in order to be more silent" (McMillan and Fehsenfeld, 229). Others have suggested that the "Old stancher" speech is Hamm's final stoic act. In it, Nagg's curse on him, his prophecy for Clov ("If he could have his child with him. . . . It was the moment I was waiting for" [*EG,* 83]), and his own prophecy ("You CRIED for night; it comes— It FALLS: now cry in darkness" [*EG,* 83]) are all explicitly or implicitly accepted (McMillan and Fehsenfeld, 190). This night's revels now are ended. In its avoidance of checkmate, the day's playing once again preserves the stalemate, to be endlessly maintained if the inevitable end for Hamm—and by extension, for us, the audience and all humanity—is to be successfully delayed.

What inferences, if any, can we draw from the play's ending? Hamm, blind and paralyzed, seems already to have made his own decision against life. "But Clov," critic Eugene Webb suggests, "still has the power to walk out into the world and possibly make a new life of his own. Until now [Clov] has lived in Hamm's orbit, seeing the world through Hamm's eyes, which can only see ashes, but if he breaks out of the orbit, as he now seems about to do, his own vision might become an entirely different one."[12] Further, Webb suggests, "To a person imprisoned within the framework of the 'old questions, the old answers' there is no hope for renewal in a world the old patterns of thought cannot fit. Clov, however, is confronted with the challenge of learning to walk out into an absurd universe, to face it, and to live in it. Whether this will work out or not Clov does not know, nor do we" (Webb, 65).

5

HAMM AND CLOV

Many characters in Beckett's plays suffer some sort of physical or psychological malady endemic in a world where yearning for anything in life—past, present, or future—is unrealistic and pointless. In *Endgame*, for example, Hamm is both blind and paralyzed, and his semicrippled servant, Clov, is unable to sit down or walk with ease. According to actor Jack MacGowran, this propensity of Beckett to dwell on human suffering and infirmity is not merely subjective: "There are people in the world, Beckett has discovered, who do suffer from these kinds of things, and yet they're related [like Hamm and Clov], they're married to each other—in a love-hate relationship, maybe" (Gontarski, 222–23). Although Beckett, over the years, frequently told MacGowran that his own childhood was, as most childhoods go, very good and very normal, he did admit that he " 'was more aware of unhappiness around [him]'—not in his own home, but just in people—'than happiness.' So," MacGowran conjectured, "the sensitive chords in Beckett's nature were attuned to the unhappiness in humankind rather than the happiness" (Gontarski, 223).

Manifestation of such awareness being continuous throughout Beckett's characterizations in both fiction and drama, MacGowran further states:

> When Beckett gave up teaching French at Trinity College, Dublin, he left suddenly, because, as he said to me, he felt he was teaching something he knew nothing about. That decision was the birth of a writer. He came to London and took a job as an attendant in a mental home for a year. That influenced him very much—I know that *Murphy,* his first novel, came out of his experiences as a mental attendant. And, then, he has seen many people who were handicapped severely in some way. When he was young, there was a war pensioners' hospital very close to where he was born. He saw them regularly every day—they were in various stages of physical disability. I am sure these experiences have influenced the fact that his characters are largely damaged people. (Gontarski, 223)

Such early personal experience may very well have inspired the "damaged people" who constitute *Endgame*'s cast of characters—Hamm, Clov, Nagg, and Nell; their will to struggle against odds devoid of hope is made remarkable by the insuperable handicaps, both physical and psychological, with which they are burdened.

During rehearsals of various *Endgame* productions that Beckett himself directed, he occasionally let drop to actors significant comments about Hamm and Clov that he never seemed willing to share with curious journalists, critics, and scholars, seeking information about the play. On one occasion, for instance, he was reported to have said that the decrepit Hamm and Clov are really "Vladimir and Estragon [the protagonists of *Godot*] at the end of their lives" (Bair, 468); on another occasion, he "qualified this remark, stating that Hamm and Clov were actually himself and Suzanne [his wife] as they were in the 1950's—when they found it difficult to stay together but impossible to leave each other" (Bair, 468). On still another occasion, Beckett was reported to have told Patrick Magee, who played Hamm in a London production, that he had no idea what went on in Hamm's mind: " 'You're on your own to figure that one out, Pat,' he said. When Magee asked Beckett to tell him how he envisioned Hamm, Beckett replied without pausing, 'Oh, he's a monster, not a human being. Only the monster remains.' But this remark seemed to frighten Beckett, and he softened it by saying, 'No, no, he looks like you, Pat. Just like you'" (Bair, 468).

In 1967, when directing *Endspiel* (the German version of *Endgame*) in Berlin, Beckett said to Ernst Schroeder, the German actor playing Hamm, "[Hamm] is a king in this chess match lost from the start. From the start he knows he is making loud senseless moves. That he will make no progress at all with the gaff. Now at the last he makes a few senseless moves as only a bad player would. A good one would have given up long ago. He is only trying to delay the inevitable end. Each of his gestures is one of the last useless moves which put off the end. He's a bad player" (Cohn 1973, 152). Critics have responded variously to these remarks. Ruby Cohn observes that Hamm "is a bad player because he is a good performer; the show must go on" (Cohn 1973, 152). Herbert Blau suggests that Hamm, in his blind and paralyzed condition, brings to mind Monsieur Argan, Molière's Imaginary Invalid, which ironically was the very role Molière himself played on the night of his death, 17 February 1673; Monsieur Argan, like Hamm, is "given to an excess of that self-dramatization which [similarly] mars and aggrandizes the Shakespearean hero; like Othello or Lear, [Hamm] savors his grief and his role" (Gontarski, 270).

To Beckett, it is Hamm who, in saying "no to nothingness" (Cohn 1973, 152) despite his insuperable handicaps, is the constant energizing force and presence in the play, Clov merely serving as an instrument of his will. Clov can in fact, be seen as Hamm's means of keeping the dying world still in motion and of staving off the end which he fears (McMillan and Fehsenfeld, 218). Further, Clov, in contrast, has only one motivation, his definition of survival: "to get back into his kitchen—[and] that must be always evident, just like Hamm's constant effort to [detain] him" (McMillan and Fehsenfeld, 218–20). Moreover, as Beckett has clearly stipulated, "There must be maximum aggression between [Hamm and Clov] from [their] first exchange of words onward. Their war is the nucleus of the play" (McMillan and Fehsenfeld, 205), creating a general mood or spirit of "extreme anxiety": "Hamm is afraid Clov might leave him. At the same time, he must be afraid that Clov will be able to find a life for himself outside

ENDGAME

the [shelter], and also that Clov might find nothing but a terrible void [which would confirm Hamm's worst fear]" (Bair, 468). It is this clash of will between technical servant and technical master that creates the central energy and suspense of the play that can grab and hold an audience's rapt attention throughout the action. As Beckett himself remarked to critic Alec Reid, "In *Godot,* the audience wonders if Godot will ever come; in *Endgame,* it wonders if Clov will ever leave."[1]

Hamm's character and plight, like those of many tragic protagonists, are capable of arousing both pity and fear in audiences and readers. Blind, paralyzed, and humiliatingly dependent on Clov, Hamm is as terrified by his own impotence as he is determined to hide it from the other three occupants of the shelter. Like an aged lion, he must roar the sounds of tyrannical authority and scorn to hide his own lost power, confidence, and self-assurance. Clov, his only life support, "makes Hamm try to be friendly to him, but then always causes [Hamm] to find refuge in a tyrannical attitude" (McMillan and Fehsenfeld, 210–11). Secretly, Hamm also fears his dying parents, Nagg and Nell, who serve as both a painful reminder of physical deterioration and an unwitting evidence of his total inability to feel even care or concern for his elders. His affected scorn of them does not make him invulnerable to their impotent rage, or to the parental curse of Nagg's "Yes, I hope I'll live till then, to hear you calling me like when you were a tiny boy, and were frightened, in the dark, and I was your only hope" (*EG,* 56).

To distract himself from such fears and threats, and to continue his reign as handicapped master of the handicapped Clov, Nagg, and Nell, Hamm engrosses himself whenever possible in routine self-dramatization. To critic Jan Kott, the blind, paralyzed, catheterized, and armchair-ridden Hamm brings to mind "a degraded and powerless tyrant, a 'ruin'd piece of nature.' He [is] a King Lear in the scene in Act IV, where Lear meets the blind Gloucester and after a great frantic monologue gives the order that one of his shoes be taken off, as it pinches."[2] To further extend this Shakespearean analogy, Clov can be seen as the clownish Fool to Hamm's Lear, but with a significant difference. Clov, as Kott suggests, is a clown who is more unhappy than his master, for unlike Hamm, Clov has yet to realize the folly of all suffering, and so is more resigned than resistant to his fated servitude. A fool, moreover, "who has accepted the fact that he is only a jester in the service of the prince, ceases to be a clown. . . . [T]he clown's philosophy is based on the assumption that everyone is a fool; and the greatest fool is he who does not know he is a fool: the prince himself. That is why the clown has to make fools of others; otherwise he would not be a clown" (Kott, 120). Clov enjoys making a fool of "the prince himself," Hamm. Whenever possible, he consciously compensates for his servile obedience by performing routine duties with either calculated recalcitrance or purposeful defiance of Hamm's specific instructions. Clov, according to Jack MacGowran, "takes an insane delight in saying, 'There's no more pain-killer,' and when he wheels Hamm to the center [of the room], he doesn't wheel him to the center. Clov is constantly *not* doing what Hamm wants him to do. Hamm[, however,] knows he's not in the center; he has a sixth sense for knowing" (Gontarski, 218). Further, MacGowran suggests, Hamm "places a terrible curse on Clov when he says, 'One day you'll be blind like me . . . except that you won't have anyone with you.' This hurts Clov; this worries him a lot. So they hurt each other mentally. They're mentally both very damaged people anyway" (Gontarski, 218).

To this interpretation of Clov's behavior, Beckett's own commentary offers details very helpful to an actor playing the role. Clov, for example, may represent human "creative intelligence, the strung-up 'eyes' of Hamm. Toward Hamm, the blind crippled will, [Clov] displays a cruel, respectful distance" (McMillan and Fehsenfeld, 181). The actor portraying Clov, ideally, should be thin, skinny, and nervous in nature, and must never touch Hamm at any time during the action of the play, as a means of establishing both literal and figurative isolation of the two characters from each other (McMillan and Fehsenfeld, 232). Also, since Clov "holds Hamm responsible for everything connected with death" (McMillan and Fehsenfeld, 232), he is indignant at Hamm's inquiry as to whether or not his old doctor is dead: "*You* ask me that?" (McMillan and Fehsenfeld, 232).

Despite the recurrent motif of Clov's constant attempts to reach the doorway leading to both his kitchen and the outside world, in the final version of the script, Clov, dressed for the road, stands impassive and motionless in the doorway throughout the last scene. As Hamm delivers his final speech, Clov's loyalty to himself and to his habit of obedience to Hamm traps him in an almost Hamletian dilemma. Paralyzed by his indecision about whether to leave or not to leave, his paralysis may in itself constitute an unconscious decision to stay. To actor Jack MacGowran, who played Clov in several productions of *Endgame,* the reason Clov doesn't leave at the end is that "Hamm puts a doubt into his mind whether he does see life outside [the shelter] or not. If he did see life outside, Clov would escape, and Hamm wouldn't worry because he would take in the new life [the small boy whom Clov claims to have seen with his telescope] to help him. . . . Hamm says, 'I don't need you any more.' Clov doesn't like the fact that he's not needed—he must be needed. That is why he never leaves" (Gontarski, 217). Further, "Clov will not go because he cannot face what's outside without anybody. He's achieved one thing: He will not answer the whistle any more. But he's still dependent upon Hamm no matter what happens" (Gontarski, 217).

Critics Martin Esslin and Theodor Adorno identify possible common-noun origins of the names of Hamm, Clov, Nagg, and Nell. Hamm, for example, may be an abbreviation of the German word *Hammer;* Clov may derive from the French *clou,* a nail; and both Nagg and Nell may derive from the German *Naegel* (nail) and the Middle English *naile,* respectively. To critic Ruby Cohn, *Endgame* "abounds in animal associations: Hamm is an edible part of pig, and Clov either is spice accompaniment, or perhaps a reference to the cloven-hoofed animals which, pigs excepted, were the only permissible meat for biblical Jews. A nag is a small horse, and Nell a common name for horse; Nagg-nag and Nell-knell are puns as well" (Cohn 1962, 229). Further, Cohn suggests, "Hamm refers to Clov as his dog, and Clov makes a toy dog for Hamm. Clov feeds Nagg Spratt's medium animal biscuits. An off-stage rat and an on-stage flea are objects of Clov's murderous intent, for rather than propagate all species, Nagg's progeny, Hamm and (perhaps) Clov, seek to extinguish them" (Cohn 1962, 229). Cohn also cites "the off-stage Mother Pegg, for a 'peg' is also a nail," adding that the "Latin *Hamus* is hook, a kind of crooked nail, so that Hamm may be viewed as another nail. In this sense, every proper name in *Endgame* is a nail, and 'nailhood' seems sardonically to symbolize humanity, whose role is to nail Christ to the Cross. All the characters are thus instruments working towards the play's paradoxical opening word, 'Finished'" (Cohn 1962, 233).

Ham was also in the Bible, Noah's second son, traditionally the ancestory of African peoples (Genesis 10:6–20). Further, just as Hamm's double *mm* suggests ancient Babylonia's King Hammurabi, who promulgated a system of laws, called the Code of Hammurabi, that included "an eye for an eye, a tooth for a tooth," so does Clov suggest King Clovis, founder of the French monarchy, or his son Clovis, who was reduced to servile labor. And *Endgame* being game, of course, there is also the suggestion of the garlic clove to season food and the spice clove, derived from the dried flower bud of a tropical evergreen tree of the myrtle family, also used to season food as well as preserve old meat.

Beckett once described *Endgame* as a "cantata for two voices" (McMillan and Fehsenfeld, 163), a musical composition consisting of vocal solos, choruses, and so forth, used as a setting for a story to be sung but not acted. Hamm and Clov presumably provide the two voices, and Nagg and Nell the occasional choral interludes. But given the derivation of each of the four characters' names from, among other things, various words meaning "nail," one could also describe Beckett's dramatic composition—as Ernst Schroeder, who played Hamm in the 1967 Berlin production of *Endspiel* has done—as "a play for a hammer and three nails" (McMillan and Fehsenfeld, 238).

6

NAGG AND NELL

Deteriorating with age as well as literally legless as the result of a tandem-bicycle accident in the Ardennes region in their past, Hamm's dying parents, Nagg and Nell, have been permanently consigned, presumably by Hamm, to two dirty old battered ashbins for the remainder of their dwindling lives. Though their roles are, compared with those of Hamm and Clov, peripheral in the play, their physical plight, coupled with their cruel ashbin imprisonment—in itself a grotesque and striking image—has inspired many to describe or refer to *Endgame* simply as the "ashbin play."

When once asked about a particular French production of *Fin de partie*, why Nagg and Nell are consigned to ashbins, Beckett replied, "It was simply a question of logistics" (Bair, 469). His statement is further amplified by his biographer, Deirdre Bair:

> Technically it was the only feasible way to have [Nagg and Nell] make their abrupt but unobtrusive entrances and exits. Originally, [Beckett] had planned to have them in wheelchairs, but it was evident even before rehearsals began that their chairs would detract from Hamm's mood of magnificent isolation that was to dominate

the stage. More important, they were to be aged and infirm, incapable of pushing themselves on or off the stage. Who, then, was to push them, and how were they to be pushed without colliding with Hamm or forcing him to move or to be moved? . . . "I put them there[, Beckett said,] so they can pop their heads up and down as needed, and nothing else is called for." (Bair, 469)

It seems very apparent, however, from the play's text that Beckett's personal feelings for these two helpless ashbin occupants are of deep compassion, if not loving tenderness, symbolizing as they do any dispossessed and discarded older generation. Jack MacGowran, when interviewed by Richard Toscan in 1973, confirms the impression that Hamm's harsh mistreatment of his parents does indeed reflect "the way most of us, in later life, treat our own parents—we put them into homes and we give them the minimum kind of treatment to keep them alive for as long as we can. The human race generally does that to an aging parent and this was [Beckett's] conception of how stark it could be—putting them into [ashbins] and giving them a biscuit or a biscuit and a half a day, anything to keep them going just for a while" (Gontarski, 219).

In addition to their obvious infirmities, Nagg and Nell suffer from sight and hearing loss as well as hunger, chill, and chronic drowsiness, which inflame their impotent rage toward Hamm. Presumably it is also Hamm who has assigned Clov the routine task of winding each of the ashbins in old sheets at night, and unwinding them in the morning. This is the ritual that opens and closes the play.

Though Nagg and Nell's roles are neither as extensive nor as demanding as those of Hamm and Clov, they are distinctly difficult. According to Beckett, they must never look at each other, even when they attempt to kiss ("A little kiss"—"Try" [*EG*, 14]), and must speak their dialogue quickly and "without color" (McMillan and Fehsenfeld, 209–10), except when fondly recalling romantic memories of their past. Moreover, all that remains of their mobility is a bare hint of an inclination of their bodies, while their eyes remain fixed straight forward, even, for example, in their dialogue exchanges such as ("Can you see me?"—"Poorly"). Beckett purposefully forgoes realism here in favor of a total effect of quiescence (McMillan and Fehsenfeld, 210). Providing *Endgame*'s subplot, Nagg and Nell speak of the past in almost exclusively short lines and very simple words. And when Nell, for example, recalls once being happy, Nagg challenges her memory, claiming she used to laugh, not because she was happy, but because he told good jokes (Cohn 1973, 147). Further, according to Beckett, both Nagg and Nell "must arrive perfectly upon the note of rigidity of old age, in which life is the burning out of a distant memory" (McMillan and Fehsenfeld, 210). To underscore this impression, Beckett would also like the old couple's "entries" from their individual ashbins (which literally hold them physically upright) to suggest a kind of " 'macabre epiphany': first their hands appear, grasping the rims of their respective ashbins, then their heads push up the lids, and as soon as their shoulders become visible, they must cease movement" (McMillan and Fehsenfeld, 210).

Critic Sidney Homan (who perceives Clov as actor to Hamm's role as playwright) contends that Nagg and Nell view the present as nothing more than a "farce." "Their sight, both physical and artistic (visionary)," according to Homan, "is going; even the sand in the bottom of their ashbins is not the procreative seashore sand . . . but only a cheap substitute for the much-preferred sawdust."[1] In contrast with Hamm and Clov, Homan further contends, "Nagg—'nagging,' even as the name Nell suggests, among other things, death's 'knell'—has lost his son, both by his anger at Hamm's ingratitude and by Hamm's own incompatibility with an unimaginative old man. In this way Nagg and Nell represent a play within the play, the countermovement to what [Homan perceives] as the procreative, romantic relationship (however strained) between Hamm and Clov and—at length—the audience" (Homan, 68). Further, Homan perceptively notes, Nagg and Nell are one of the few couples with dialogue in Beckett's plays who actually "die" and "who have lost even more than their mobility. [To be sure,] Hamm has lost his [mobility too], but that loss is only a springboard to the cultivation of an inner vision. [Nagg and Nell's] movement, however, is a constrictive one from a vaguely romantic past, to tales

unwanted and unappreciated by Nagg, to a craving for physical com-
forts that only mocks their imprisonment, to silence, and at length
extinction" (Homan, 68). Moreover, according to Homan, Nagg has a
curious need for Nell to be an attentive audience for his stories, even
though she protests the role. If we think, however, of Nagg and Nell
forming with us, the audience, "the other half of a theater-in-the-
round, then [the old couple] are our own reverse images. Like us they
are confined to seats, a captive audience, even if that comparison is a
bit bizarre. However, in moving from a potentially significant, surely
happier past to their own isolated, present [and pressing] physical
wants, they may at length alienate us" (Homan, 70).

Though Beckett acknowledged that his favorite line in *Endgame*
is Hamm's response to Clov's observation that Nagg is crying—"Then
he's living" (Cohn 1973, 154)—he identified the most important sentence in the play as being Nell's remark that "Nothing is funnier than
unhappiness, I grant you that" (Cohn 1973, 154). In 1967, when
Beckett staged *Endgame* in German translation in Berlin, he directed it
so as to emphasize its sardonic display of the fun of unhappiness as
well as the point of the play's title.

Last, critic David Helsa perceptively notes, discernible in
Endgame's dramatic structure are at least five metaphoric dimensions
that are also graphically physicalized in Beckett's carefully conceived
and described stage setting of the play. At one and the same time, the
stage set represents a chessboard in the final moments of play, the
throne room of a dying king, a stage set on which the final scene of a
drama is being enacted, the study of a writer who no longer is able to
create, and the interior of the skull of a man who is dying of dichoto-
my. Moreover, Helsa contends, "Ruby Cohn is surely correct in urging
that the stage also represents a Golgotha; and we may perhaps also see
in it a prison and a man condemned to die in a gas chamber or an elec-
tric chair" (Helsa, 154–55).

In itemizing these five metaphoric dimensions, Helsa suggests,
further, that their common and unifying theme—and hence that of the
play overall—is the fulfillment of Clov's dream: "A world where all
would be silent and still and each thing in its last place, under the last

dust" (*EG*, 57). To Helsa, "Time is over for kings and actors and writers and all who play the game of human existence. It is the end of the Self whose body and mind we have seen continually abrading each other. It is the end of the World which lies on the other side of those hollow bricks which represent Skull" (Helsa, 155).

7

FURTHER PERSPECTIVES

In 1988, Harold Bloom, Sterling Professor of the Humanities at Yale University, edited and introduced a recent collection of eight essays on *Endgame* for Chelsea House Publishers' Modern Critical Interpretations series. Three of these eight essays—Hugh Kenner's "Life in the Box," Antony Easthope's "Hamm, Clov, and Dramatic Method in *Endgame*," and Theodor W. Adorno's "Towards an Understanding of *Endgame*"—had previously been anthologized in *Twentieth Century Interpretations of "Endgame"* (1969), edited by Bell Gale Chevigny, and a brief summary of each has been included in chapter 3 of this study. The remaining five essays anthologized in Bloom's 1988 collection, each of which offers other, equally insightful perspectives by which *Endgame* may be viewed, will be briefly summarized in this chapter.

Stanley Cavell, in "Ending the Waiting Game: A Reading of Beckett's *Endgame*" (1969), presents a detailed interpretation that views Hamm, Clov, Nagg, and Nell as Noah and his family in their arklike shelter sometime after the Flood. The principal focus of Cavell's analysis, however, is on the seeming *ordinariness* of the play's events and on the *hidden literality* of the language and grammar of its dialogue. *Endgame*'s language, Cavell suggests, "sounds as extraordinary as its people look, but it imitates, as Chekhov's does, the qualities of ordinary conversation among people whose world is shared—catching shades of memory, regret, intimidation; its opacity to the outsider. It is an abstract imitation, where Chekhov's is objective."[1] Nevertheless, Cavell contends, "it is an achievement for the theater, to my mind, of the same magnitude. Not, of course, that the imitation of the ordinary is the only, or best, option for writing dialogue. Not every dramatist wants this quality; a writer like Shakespeare can get it whenever he wants it. But to insist upon the ordinary, keep its surface and its rhythm, sets a powerful device" (Bloom, 62). Further, Cavell contends, "To miss the ordinariness of the lives in *Endgame* is to avoid the extraordinariness (and ordinariness) of our own" (Bloom, 62).

Richard Gilman, in his essay entitled "Beckett," explores Beckett's decision to turn from fiction to drama and the close relationship that exists between his fiction and his plays, focusing specifically on *Waiting for Godot* and *Endgame*. Gilman then goes on to explore Beckett's conscious elimination of extraneous detail in his later plays, such as *Krapp's Last Tape* (1958) and *Play* (1963), in which human experience is distilled to the irreducible essence of a mere response to being alive. In regard to *Endgame* in particular, Gilman suggests that it demonstrates "how our self-dramatizing impulses, our need for building Ibsen's castles, is inseparable from the content of our experiences, how we do not in fact know our experience except in literary or histrionic terms. And this is independent of whether the experience is solemn or antic, exalted or base" (Bloom, 85). Further, Gilman suggests, "We give [experience] reality and dignity by expressing it, we validate it by finding, or rather hopelessly seeking, the 'right' words and forms. This is what is going on in *Endgame* beneath the lugubriousness and anomie: 'Something is taking its course,' Clov says, not their lives—they are actors, they have no 'lives'—but their filling in of the emptiness with their drama" (Bloom, 85).

Paul Lawley, in his essay entitled "Symbolic Structure and Creative Obligation in *Endgame*," presents a close examination of the symbolic organization in the play and of how visual imagery and language function together to create both meaning and myth. *Endgame*,

Lawley contends, "is concerned not just with a terminal world but with the survival of the perceiving and creating self [Hamm] within a terminal world."[2] Further, Lawley contends, when we look at *Endgame*'s stage setting, we are in fact observing a "visual image of the function of language in the play. In a world in which invention, fictional creation, is . . . always tending to become absolute and all forms tend towards abstraction, language, the only remaining creative medium, ceases to function as a medium, a tool or instrument for organizing and making sense of the perceptions of an external world, and becomes instead a separate self-sufficient structure in the midst of the alien environment" (Lawley, 56). Lawley concludes that *Endgame* "works by indirection: image, symbol, narrative, gesture and echo all converge patiently on a center which is, like Hamm himself, unstable, indefinable, perhaps even nonexistent" (Lawley, 68).

In her Beckett study, *Just Play: Beckett's Theater* (1980), Ruby Cohn includes a highly informative chapter on *Endgame* entitled "The Play That Was Rewritten: *Fin de partie*." In it, she examines in detail the multidraft, extensively revised evolution *Fin de partie* (*Endgame*) underwent in the two years that Beckett painstakingly labored over it. She concludes her discussion by focusing on Hamm's erroneous remark that the day of the play's action is no different from any other for him. "It is *not* like any other day," Cohn argues, "for only on this day are there 'no more' things, from bicycle-wheels to coffins. Only on this day does Clov sight a small boy and propose to leave. It is only this unending day that Beckett stages, with the symmetries and repetitions that *seem* to support Hamm's conclusion—the old questions, the old answers, the old moves, the old pauses."[3] Further, Cohn argues, "This day and only this day is distinguished by its brave comic play against a background of tragic waning, but Beckett's skill—exercised in revision—leaves us with Hamm's impression. Hamm is wrong about the insignificance of the day, but he is right to worry about 'beginning to mean something.' For Beckett has revised *Endgame* into its present meaningful economy" (Cohn 1980, 186).

Sidney Homan, in his Beckett study *Beckett's Theaters: Interpretations for Performance* (1984), includes a chapter entitled "*Endgame:* The Playwright Completes Himself," which focuses on the play's four characters and their complementary, yet uneasy, relationship with each other. Clov, Homan suggests, "must war with Hamm, actor with playwright, because Clov, constitutionally unlike the playwright, can assert his integrity only as a reverse image of his master's" (Homan, 64). To Homan, Nagg and Nell represent, in one sense, "a horrible extension of Clov's unimaginative mentality. Their demands are not for the food of a playwright, but for their own 'pap'; . . . [these] parents are nothing more than creatures of pressing and present physical desire: to eat, to be scratched, to make love as best they can in the ashbins" (Homan, 67). In contrast with Clov, Nagg, and Nell, Homan sees Hamm as both a god and an artist (playwright) from whom the other three characters derive their identity and sustenance. Given the various stories recounted in the play, Homan suggests, "Hamm is his own story and storyteller, the narrator/narrated, spinning his tales spiderlike from within himself. . . . As Hamm says, 'There's no one else,' and in his way Hamm embodies all people: he is the man seeking bread, and the object of that charity, and the stern judge who denies succor, and Mother Pegg who, like Socrates, seeks truth with her light, as well as Mother Pegg barely existing in her final days with that light extinguished" (Homan, 62). Further, Homan suggests, "In a sense [*Endgame*] is one large monologue parading as a four-character drama. Like Shakespeare's Richard II in his cell, Hamm peoples his little world through his union of heart and head—his equivalent for that coupling of mind and soul in his royal counterpart" (Homan, 68).

This selection of five alternative perspectives on *Endgame* is, of course, only representative of various recent examples of traditional critical approaches to Beckett's play. It would be grossly incomplete without some acknowledgment, or at least some token example, of the various nontraditional approaches to literature that are currently generating so much scholarly attention and activity both here in the United States and abroad. Sylvie Debevec Henning, for example, in her study entitled *Beckett's Critical Complicity: Carnival, Contestation, and Tradition* (1988), includes a provocative hermeneutical analysis of *Endgame* that exemplifies at least one of the directions Beckett scholarship and criticism may be going in the future. In her analysis, Henning proposes that in *Endgame,* "as perhaps in all of Beckett's work, the text itself reproduces [on several levels] a contest [between those forces which strive for a full, harmonious unification and those which contest against it]. In the explicit narrative, Hamm and Clov struggle to deny the indeterminacy of their 'messy' condition. Yet, it keeps returning to increase their anguish."[4] Henning also suggests that Hamm and Clov, at the same time, "endeavor to eradicate crucial aspects of the carnivalesque—the body, nature, time, history, laughter—whenever they manifest themselves. A similar act of double repression is repeated on the stylistic level, where an effort at straightforward monovocality and orderliness is countered by the processes of linguistic dissemination that cannot be contained" (Henning, 87–88). Further, Henning proposes, "On all levels, the carnivalesque both counteracts the totalizing impetus and interacts with it in an agon that contributes greatly to the palpable tension of the play. *Endgame* is largely a comment upon similar confrontations that have repeatedly occurred throughout the course of Western history" (Henning, 88). Moreover, Henning proposes, *Endgame,* by the very act of testing and contesting our familiar teleological hermeneutics, "may, in the uncertainty of its own nature, be demonstrating and providing, not simply a critique, but an alternative as well" (Henning, 88).

Endgame will no doubt continue to inspire other equally thought-provoking interpretations such as these. And one can only wonder what new or different light future critical theories and approaches to drama may shed on our present understanding and appreciation of Beckett's remarkable, yet enigmatic, "ashbin play."

8

ODDS AND ENDINGS

The overall running time of *Endgame* in performance is some 85 minutes. During that time, Clov's 16 entrances and 16 exits are verbally challenged by Hamm 26 times. Five times Clov appears on command of Hamm's whistle-call, moving to his place next to Hamm's armchair four times and remaining in the doorway once. Four of his other 11 appearances are motivated by his need for some object either verbally identified ("I'm back again with . . .") or silently provided. These "object entrances," as Michael Haerdter calls them in his *Endspiel* rehearsal diary (1967) (McMillan and Fehsenfeld, 235), punctuate the play from beginning to end.

Another indication of formal principles of control in *Endgame* is Beckett's deliberate use of repetition, as gradually revealed in the play's script and subsequently emphasized in his own direction of it. There are virtually no changes in the shelter enclosure occupied by the four characters, or in their respective dispositions:

> All changes are immobilised as reminiscences: ("Do you remember— . . . when we crashed on our tandem and lost our shanks," asks Nagg) or stamped with the seal of appearance: (Hamm, showing interest in Nell: "Go and see is she dead"; Clov: "Looks

like it"), or else transposed into a vague future: (Hamm to Clov: "One day you'll be blind, like me"). Time stands still on stage. Beckett's characters have only one desire, to escape the oppressive presence of time. But then boredom and weariness always gain the upper hand again, and point the tedious way to the "end" before their eyes. Hamm gloomily: "Then it's a day like any other day." Clov: "As long as it lasts. (Pause) All life long, the same inanities." They are acting out a game, playing repeated "roles" for all eternity. (McMillan and Fehsenfeld, 214–15)

In his essay entitled "Symbolic Stillness and Creative Obligation in *Endgame,*" critic Paul Lawley perceptively notes Beckett's overall strategy in the play: "The game is language, and the play is about the struggle with this inevitably defunct tool of perception and survival" (Lawley, 53). Words and images, Lawley notes, tyrannize Clov just as they tyrannize the play's spectators, who bring their own illusions of false realities with them to the performance. Moreover, in section 11 of the play, Beckett reinforces this strategy by almost going so far as to dare the audience to leave the theater: when Clov asks Hamm what is there in the shelter to keep him from leaving, Hamm promptly replies, "the dialogue" (EG, 58). Lawley also notes that Hamm has learned an "endgame" of words, to which he is "no less subject to the tyranny of language than his own slave. . . . Language used to be Hamm's slave; he 'invented' it, used it to build himself a refuge that would protect him from the devastated outside and taught it to his slaves" (Lawley, 58).

Building on Lawley's theory, critic Gordon S. Armstrong suggests that Hamm and Clov may actually represent language and movement, respectively, and once words and actions are abolished on stage—as they are in section 16—the drama ceases to exist. To Armstrong, the play, for Beckett as for his audience, "does not end with the words and actions dispensed. 'You'—that indefinable presence of the within— 'remain.' The cloven feet and the hammy mouth are gone, signalling consciousness's freedom from the tyranny of words and actions."[1] Further, Armstrong suggests that this "does not limit the communicative content of *Endgame,* although it might be argued that Beckett's solution effectively ends this play's game of words and actions in the external sphere of things. But the game begins anew when Hamm removes the handkerchief from his eyes" (Armstrong, 48).

In his essay entitled "Chess with the Audience: Samuel Beckett's *Endgame*," critic James Acheson proposes the theory that the play's circular structure as a whole suggests "a routine endlessly repeated by the four characters in order to pass the time. It is part of the routine for Hamm and Nagg to tell their stories over and over again; and it is significant that in *his* story, Hamm identifies with the narrator/feudal overlord, who has power of life and death over other people."[2] To Acheson, however, Hamm's aspirations to godhead are essentially pointless: "aware of the brevity and meaninglessness of life, and of the need to palliate what Beckett has called 'the suffering of being,' Hamm assumes throughout his chess game with death a thinly-veiled pretense of power. He is joined in the game by the other characters, who are also aware of being fated to lose; and who, in pretending to a power they lack, resist Hamm's attempts to dominate them" (Acheson, 90).

Martin Esslin, in *The Theatre of the Absurd* (1969), notes that "*Endgame* . . . has a very deep and direct impact, which can spring only from its touching a chord in the minds of a very large number of human beings" (Esslin 1969, 47). Acheson concurs with Esslin, and believes, further, that *Endgame* must surely touch at least two chords: "a deeply-felt sense that the characters' impotence in the face of death—the certainty that they will lose their chess game—is something all of us share; and a sense, too, that the game Beckett plays against us is the game we play against the world and our minds all our lives long—and are, again, inevitably fated to lose" (Acheson, 190).

Moreover, in his dramatic depiction of Hamm's plight, Beckett has indeed created one of the most graphic metaphors or objective correlatives in modern drama of old age and its accompanying physical and emotional indignities. Blind, paralyzed, and catheterized, Hamm is sentenced to solitary confinement both within the claustrophobic shelter and within his own deteriorating body. The physical agility and emotional responsiveness he (presumably) once took for granted have all but deserted him. As a result, he is condemned to endure unrelentingly the dubious blessing and curse accorded those fortunate to live beyond middle age. Though outwardly he flaunts a self-confident arrogance often associated with youth (Behold! I alone am alive! I alone matter!), inwardly Hamm is painfully aware of his own precarious mortality and (perhaps even) a deep sense of irretrievable loss. His daily, blustering performance has become his sole means of defiance against his present state of physical helplessness as well as death's inevitability. At his core, Hamm may sense a poignant regret for the irrecoverable past as well as a sad surprise that he feels these losses so little. How transitory, it may come home to him, are the most intense emotions. But above all, he is predominantly consumed by a bewildering, terrifying awe at the precariousness of the whole tragic destiny of humanity when seen in the light of his own impending death.

Playwright and critic Lionel Abel, in *The Intellectual Follies: A Memoir of the Literary Venture in New York and Paris* (1984), notes that what the theater of the absurd movement—and by inclusion, Beckett—had to offer was, first, "a widespread discontent with political leaders, social institutions, the manners and morals of the time. And, secondly, resting on this reaction to events, policies, and purposes put forward in society, there was the development, not of a new logical form, but of a new feeling for the negation of logic—for illogic, for the absurd, as if it were a different or new logic."[3] Abel also notes that during this critical postwar period, "society wanted playwrights to give it something negative, and the playwrights responded, the best of them adding something extra of beauty or precision of language, as in the best works of Beckett or Pinter" (Abel, 231). Further, Abel points out, "You cannot give a theater audience anything at all if you do not give it what it wants and expects. You can give it more besides, but you cannot only give them this more besides. Beckett . . . gave audiences the negations they wanted to hear and a beauty of language and feeling they did not expect, a plus in addition to the minus they had come to the theater to get" (Abel, 231).

Martin Esslin, in *Mediations: Essays on Brecht, Beckett, and the Media* (1980), observes that "No writer of our time has more consistently refused to comment on or explain his own work than Beckett. Yet no writer of our time has provoked a larger volume of critical comment, explanation, and exegesis in so short a time. It is hard, in working one's way through the numerous articles, reviews, essays, and weighty volumes of criticism that have appeared about him, to keep in mind how very recent and rapid his rise to world fame has been."[4] Further, Esslin observes, "Beckett's reticence is no mere whim. Inevitably, there exists an organic connection between his refusal to explain his meaning . . . and the critics' massive urge to supply an explanation. Indeed, it might be argued that in that correlation between the author's and the critics' attitudes lies one of the keys to the whole phenomenon of Samuel Beckett, his *oeuvre,* and its impact" (Esslin 1980, 75–76).

"In Beckett's work," Esslin contends,

> this tension between the transient, unendingly decaying nature of the material universe and the immaterial aspect of consciousness, which incessantly renews itself in ever recurring self-perception, plays an important part. Consciousness cannot conceive of itself as nonexisting and is therefore only conceivable as unlimited, without end. The more in Beckett's works the material envelope decays and is stripped away, the more painful becomes the tension between the temporal and the infinite. Beckett's characters may lose the capacity for locomotion; their senses may decay; yet their awareness of their own self continues relentlessly; and time can never have a stop: the final situations in *Waiting for Godot,* in *Endgame,* or in *How It Is,* imply eternal recurrence, while in *Play* it is probably the impossibility of an extinction of consciousness through death itself that is dramatized: as the individual can never become aware of his own cessation, his final moments of consciousness must remain, as it were, eternally suspended in limbo and can be conceived as recurring through all eternity. (Esslin 1980, 83)

Through such dramatic masterpieces as *Waiting for Godot* and *Endgame,* Beckett has achieved a worldwide impact that is both profound and without counterpart in twentieth-century drama. "His plays stay in the bones," director Alan Schneider once observed. "His words strike to the marrow—the sudden sharp anguish of . . . a Hamm crying out for understanding in an uncertain universe; Clov's detailed description of the bleak harsh landscape of our existence on earth. While against and in spite of the harshness and the uncertainty, there is the constant assertion of man's will, and spirit, his sense of humor, as the only bulwarks against despair; the constant 'glimmers of hope,' even in the dark depths of that abyss in which we find ourselves" (Chevigny, 21).

In awarding the Nobel Prize in Literature to Beckett in 1969, the secretary of the Swedish Academy aptly spoke of his "combination of paradox and mystery, containing a love of mankind that grows in understanding as it plumbs farther into the depths of abhorrence, a courage of despair, a compassion that has to reach the utmost of suffering to discover that there are no bounds of charity." *Endgame,* perhaps more than any other of Beckett's plays, embodies this "combination of paradox and mystery," and in Hamm and Clov's perpetual stalemate Beckett makes immediate and compelling to us, as audience or reader, our own constant efforts to assert will, spirit, and humor in defiance of despair.

Notes and References

1. Backgrounds and Influences

1. Oscar G. Brockett, *History of the Theatre* (Boston: Allyn and Bacon, 1968), 647; hereafter cited in text.

2. Edward Albee, "Which Theatre Is the Absurd One?" *New York Times Magazine,* 25 February 1962, 31; hereafter cited in text.

3. Deirdre Bair, *Samuel Beckett: A Biography* (New York and London: Harcourt Brace Jovanovich, 1978), 35; hereafter cited in text.

4. Rosette Lamont, "Two Avant-Gardists Reveal Their Classicism," *New York Times,* 19 August 1984, sec. H, p. 7.

2. The Importance of *Endgame*

1. S. E. Gontarski, *On Beckett: Essays and Criticism* (New York: Grove Press, 1986), 269; hereafter cited in text.

2. Ruby Cohn, *Samuel Beckett: The Comic Gamut* (New Brunswick, N.J.: Rutgers University Press, 1962), 228; hereafter cited in text.

3. Samuel Beckett, "Letter to Alan Schneider, 29 December 1957," in *Village Voice Reader,* ed. Daniel Wolf and Edwin Fancher (Garden City, N.Y.: Doubleday, 1962), 185.

3. Endgame's Reception

1. Kenneth Tynan, *Curtains: Selections from the Drama Criticism and Related Writings* (New York: Atheneum, 1961), 402.

2. A. J. Leventhal, "Close of Play: Reflections on Samuel Beckett's New Work for the French Theatre," *Dublin Magazine,* April–June 1957, 22.

3. John Unterecker, "Samuel Beckett's No-Man's Land," *New Leader* 42 (18 May 1959):24.

4. Alan Schneider, "Waiting for Beckett: A Personal Chronicle," *Chelsea Review* 2 (September 1958):3; hereafter cited in text.

5. Bell Gale Chevigny, ed., *Twentieth Century Interpretations of "Endgame": A Collection of Critical Essays* (Englewood, N.J.: Prentice Hall, 1969), 3; hereafter cited in text.

6. Martin Esslin, *The Theatre of the Absurd* (Garden City, N.Y.: Doubleday-Anchor, 1969), 44; hereafter cited in text.

7. Alan Schneider, *Entrances: An American Director's Journey* (New York: Viking Penguin, 1986), 246.

8. Hugh Kenner, *Samuel Beckett: A Critical Study* (Berkeley and Los Angeles: University of California Press, 1973), 165.

9. George E. Wellwarth, *The Theater of Protest and Paradox: Developments in the Avant-Garde Drama,* rev. ed. (New York: New York University Press, 1971), 56.

10. Harold Hobson, untitled review of *Fin de partie,* directed by Graham Murray for the 69 Theatre Company, Shaw Theatre, London, *London Sunday Times,* 15 July 1973, 39E.

11. Tom Bishop, "Chaikin Stages *Endgame,*" *The Beckett Circle: Newsletter of the Samuel Beckett Society* 2, no. 2 (Spring 1980), 2.

4. A Structural Analysis

1. Ruby Cohn, *Back to Beckett* (Princeton, N.J.: Princeton University Press, 1973), 152; hereafter cited in text.

2. Arturo Schwarz, *The Complete Works of Marcel Duchamp* (New York: Harry N. Abrams, 1970), 70.

3. Dougald McMillan and Martha Fehsenfeld, *Beckett in the Theatre: The Author as Practical Playwright and Director,* vol. 1 (London: John Calder, 1988; New York: Riverrun Press, 1988), 231; hereafter cited in text.

4. Roy Walker, "Love, Chess, and Death," *Twentieth Century,* 164 (December 1958), 542.

5. Charles Marowitz, "Paris Log," *Encore,* March 1962, 44.

6. Samuel Beckett, *Endgame: A Play in One Act Followed by Act without Words: A Mime for One Player* (New York: Grove Press, 1958), 1; hereafter cited in text as *EG.*

7. Michael Anderson, *Anger and Detachment: A Study of Arden, Osborne, and Pinter* (London: Pitman Publishing, 1976), 22; hereafter cited in text.

8. David H. Helsa, *The Shape of Chaos: An Interpretation of the Art of Samuel Beckett* (Minneapolis: University of Minnesota Press, 1971), 157; hereafter cited in text.

9. Charles R. Lyons, *Samuel Beckett* (New York: Grove Press, 1983), 68–69.

10. Michael Robinson, *The Long Sonata of the Dead: A Study of Samuel Beckett* (New York: Grove Press, 1969), 275–76; hereafter cited in text.

11. Kristin Morrison, "Neglected Biblical Allusions in Beckett's Plays: 'Mother Pegg' Once More," in *Samuel Beckett: Humanistic Perspectives,* ed. Morris Beja, S. E. Gontarski, and Pierre Astier (Columbus: Ohio State University Press, 1983), 93; hereafter cited in text.

12. Eugene Webb, *The Plays of Samuel Beckett* (Seattle: University of Washington Press, 1974), 65; hereafter cited in text.

5. Hamm and Clov

1. Alec Reid, *All I Can Manage, More than I Could: An Approach to the Plays of Samuel Beckett* (Chester Spring, Pa.: Dufours Editions, 1968), 71.

2. Jan Kott, *Shakespeare Our Contemporary,* trans. Boleslaw Taborski (Garden City, N.Y.: Doubleday, 1964), 114; hereafter cited in text.

6. Nagg and Nell

1. Sidney Homan, *Beckett's Theaters: Interpretations for Performance* (Lewisburg, Pa.: Bucknell University Press, 1984; London and Toronto: Associated University Presses, 1984), 68; hereafter cited in text.

7. Further Perspectives

1. Harold Bloom, ed., *Samuel Beckett's "Endgame": Modern Critical Interpretations* (New York: Chelsea House Publishers, 1988), 62; hereafter cited in text.

2. Paul Lawley, "Symbolic Stillness and Creative Obligation in *Endgame,*" *Journal of Beckett Studies* 5 (1979):54; hereafter cited in text.

3. Ruby Cohn, *Just Play: Beckett's Theater* (Princeton, N.J.: Princeton University Press, 1980), 186; hereafter cited in text.

4. Sylvie Debevec Henning, *Beckett's Critical Complicity: Carnival, Contestation, and Tradition* (Lexington: The University of Kentucky Press, 1988), 87; hereafter cited in text.

8. Odds and Endings

1. Gordon S. Armstrong, *Samuel Beckett, W. B. Yeats, and Jack Yeats: Images and Words* (Lewisburg, Pa.: Bucknell University Press, 1990; London and Toronto: Associated University Presses, 1990), 48; hereafter cited in text.

2. James Acheson, "Chess with the Audience: Samuel Beckett's *Endgame*," in *Critical Essays on Samuel Beckett,* ed. Patrick A. McCarthy (Boston: G. K. Hall, 1986), 189–90; hereafter cited in text.

3. Lionel Abel, *The Intellectual Follies: A Memoir of the Literary Venture in New York and Paris* (New York and London: W. W. Norton, 1984), 229; hereafter cited in text.

4. Martin Esslin, *Mediations: Essays on Brecht, Beckett, and the Media* (Baton Rouge: Louisiana State University Press, 1980), 75; hereafter cited in text.

Bibliography

Primary Works

Endgame is published with *Act without Words: A Mime for One Player* (New York: Grove Press, 1958). Its original French version, *Fin de partie, suivi de Acte sans paroles,* was published by Editions de Minuit, Paris, 1957.

The central bibliography for Beckett's writing and for criticism of his works to 1984 is Cathleen Culotta Andonian's *Samuel Beckett: A Reference Guide* (Boston: G. K. Hall, 1989). For more recent Beckett criticism, consult the *MLA International Bibliography.*

Most of Beckett's critical writings are collected in *Disjecta,* edited by Ruby Cohn (New York: Grove Press, 1984). The other important critical work is *Proust* (London: Chatto & Windus, 1931; reprint, New York: Grove Press, 1957).

Stage Plays

All Beckett's plays, with the exception of *Waiting for Godot, Endgame,* and *Happy Days,* have been published in the following texts: *Collected Shorter Plays of Samuel Beckett* (London: Faber & Faber, 1984) and *Collected Shorter Plays of Samuel Beckett* (New York: Grove Press, 1984). For other editions of stage plays, radio plays, screenplays, and television plays, see the following citations.

Act without Words I (Acte sans paroles I). French translation. Paris: Editions de Minuit, 1957, with *Fin de partie.* English translation. New York: Grove Press, 1958, with *Endgame.*

Act without Words II (Acte sans paroles II). French translation. Paris: Editions de Minuit, 1957. English translation. New York: Grove Press, 1960.

Breath. In *Gambit* 4, no. 16 (1969):5–9. Reprinted in *First Love and Other Shorts.* New York: Grove Press, 1974.

Catastrophe. French translation. Paris: Editions de Minuit, 1982. English translation. London: Faber & Faber, 1984. In *New Yorker,* 10 January 1983, 26–27. Reprinted in *Three Plays by Samuel Beckett.* New York: Grove Press, 1983.

Come and Go (Va et vient). French translation. Paris: Editions de Minuit, 1966. English translation. London: Calder & Boyars, 1967. Reprinted in *Cascando and Other Short Dramatic Pieces.* New York: Grove Press, 1967.

Endgame (Fin de partie). French translation. Paris: Editions de Minuit, 1957. English translation. New York: Grove Press, 1958. London: Faber & Faber, 1958.

Footfalls (Pas). English translation. New York: Grove Press, 1976. Reprinted in *Ends and Odds.* New York: Grove Press, 1976. French translation. Paris: Editions de Minuit, 1977.

Happy Days (Oh les beaux jours). English translation. New York: Grove Press, 1961. London: Faber & Faber, 1962. French translation. Paris: Editions de Minuit, 1963.

Krapp's Last Tape (La Dernière bande). English translation. London: Faber & Faber, 1959. New York: Grove Press, 1960. French translation. Paris: Editions de Minuit, 1960.

Not I (Pas moi). English translation. London: Faber & Faber, 1973. New York: Grove Press, 1974. French translation. Paris: Editions de Minuit, 1975.

Ohio Impromptu (Impromptu d'ohio). English translation. In *Rockaby and Other Short Pieces.* New York: Grove Press, 1981. French translation. In *Berceuse suivi de impromptu d'ohio.* Paris: Editions de Minuit, 1982.

A Piece of Monologue. London: Faber & Faber, 1982. In *Kenyon Review,* N.S., 1, no. 3 (Summer 1979):1–4.

Play (Comédie). French translation. Paris: Editions de Minuit, 1964. English translation. London: Faber & Faber, 1964. Reprinted in *Cascando and Other Short Dramatic Pieces.* New York: Grove Press, 1967.

Rockaby (Berceuse). English translation. New York: Grove Press, 1981. London: Faber & Faber, 1982. French translation. Paris: Editions de Minuit, 1982.

Rough for Theatre I (Fragment de théâtre) and *Rough for Theatre II.* English translation. In *Ends and Odds.* New York: Grove Press, 1976. French translation. *Theatre I* first published as *Fragment de théâtre* in *Minuit* 8 (March 1974):65–72.

Bibliography

That Time (*Cette fois*). English translation. London: Faber & Faber, 1976. In *Ends and Odds*. New York: Grove Press, 1976. French translation. Paris: Editions de Minuit, 1978.

Waiting for Godot (*En attendant Godot*). French translation. Paris: Editions de Minuit, 1952. English translation. New York: Grove Press, 1954. London: Faber & Faber, 1956.

What Where. London: Faber & Faber, 1984. In *Three Plays by Samuel Beckett*. New York: Grove Press, 1983.

Radio Plays

All That Fall (*Tous ceux qui tombent*). English translation. New York: Grove Press, 1957. London: Faber & Faber, 1957. French translation by Robert Pinget and Samuel Beckett. Paris: Editions de Minuit, 1957.

Cascando. English translation. In *Evergreen Review* 7 (May–June 1963):41–57. In *Cascando and Other Short Dramatic Pieces*. New York: Grove Press, 1967. French translation. In *Comédie et actes divers*. Paris: Editions de Minuit, 1966.

Embers (*Cendres*). English translation. In *Evergreen Review* 3 (Nov.–Dec. 1959):28–41. New York: Grove Press, 1960. London: Faber & Faber, 1960. French translation by Robert Pinget and Samuel Beckett. In *Lettres Nouvelles* 36 (1959):3–14. Reprinted in *La Dernière bande, suivi de Cendres*. Paris: Editions de Minuit, 1960. Reprint. 1968.

Rough for Radio I. As "Sketch for Radio Play," in *Stereo Headphones*, 7 (Spring 1976):3–7. In *Ends and Odds*. New York: Grove Press, 1976.

Rough for Radio II (*Pochade Radiophonique*). French translation. In *Minuit* 16 (Nov. 1975):2–12. English translation. In *Ends and Odds*. New York: Grove Press, 1976.

Words and Music (*Paroles et music*). English translation. In *Evergreen Review* 6 (Nov.–Dec. 1962):34–43. In *Cascando and Other Short Dramatic Pieces*. New York: Grove Press, 1967. French translation. In *Comédie et actes divers*. Paris: Editions de Minuit, 1966.

Screenplays

Film. London: Faber & Faber, 1967. In *Cascando and Other Short Dramatic Pieces*. New York: Grove Press, 1967. Reprinted in *Film*. New York: Grove Press, 1969.

Television Plays

". . . *but the clouds* . . ." In *Ends and Odds*. New York: Grove Press, 1976.

Eh Joe (*Dis Joe*). French translation. In *Comédie et actes divers*. Paris: Editions de Minuit, 1966. English translation. In *Eh Joe and Other Writings*.

London: Faber & Faber, 1967. Reprinted in *Cascando and Other Short Dramatic Pieces* (New York: Grove Press, 1967).

Ghost Trio. In *Ends and Odds.* New York: Grove Press, 1976.

Nacht und Traeume. In *Collected Shorter Plays of Samuel Beckett.* London: Faber & Faber, 1984. New York: Grove Press, 1984.

Quad. London: Faber & Faber, 1984.

Fiction

All Strange Away. New York: Gotham Book Mart, 1976. Reprinted in *Rockaby and Other Short Pieces.* New York: Grove Press, 1981.

Company (Compagnie). English translation. New York: Grove Press, 1980. French translation. Paris: Editions de Minuit, 1980.

Enough (Assez). French translation. Paris: Editions de Minuit, 1966. Reprinted in *Têtes-mortes.* Paris: Editions de Minuit, 1967. English translation. In *No's Knife: Collected Shorter Prose, 1945–1966.* London: Calder & Boyars, 1967.

First Love and Other Stories (Premier amour). French translation. Paris: Editions de Minuit, 1970. English translation. New York: Grove Press, 1974.

Fizzles (Pour finir encore et autre foirades). French translation. Paris: Editions de Minuit, 1976. English translation. New York: Grove Press, 1981.

From an Abandoned Work (D'un ouvrage abandonné). English translation. *Trinity News* (Dublin Weekly), 7 June 1956, 3–4. Reprinted in *No's Knife: Collected Shorter Prose, 1945–1966.* London: Calder & Boyars, 1967. French translation by Ludovic and Agnès Janvier and Samuel Beckett. Paris: Editions de Minuit, 1967. Reprinted in *Têtes-mortes.* Paris: Editions de Minuit, 1967.

How It Is (Comment c'est). French translation. Paris: Editions de Minuit, 1961. Reprint, 1969. English translation. New York: Grove Press, 1964.

Ill Seen Ill Said (Mal vu mal dit). English translation. In *New Yorker,* 5 October 1981, 48–58. Reprint. New York: Grove Press, 1981. French translation. Paris: Editions de Minuit, 1981.

Imagination Dead Imagine (Imagination morte imaginez). English translation. London: Calder & Boyars, 1965. Reprinted in *No's Knife: Collected Shorter Prose, 1945–1965.* London: Calder & Boyars, 1967. French translation. Paris: Editions de Minuit, 1965. Reprinted in *Têtes-mortes.* Paris: Editions de Minuit, 1967.

Lessness (Sans). French translation. Paris: Editions de Minuit, 1969. English translation. London: Calder & Boyars, 1970.

The Lost Ones (Le Dépeupleur). French translation. Paris: Editions de Minuit, 1970. English translation. New York: Grove Press, 1972.

Bibliography

Malone Dies (*Malone meurt*). French translation. Paris: Editions de Minuit, 1951. Reprint. 1963. English translation. New York: Grove Press, 1956. Reprinted in *Three Novels*. New York: Grove Press, 1965.

Mercier and Camier (*Mercier et Camier*). French translation. Paris: Editions de Minuit, 1970. English translation. New York: Grove Press, 1974.

Molloy. French translation. Paris: Edition de Minuit, 1951. Reprint. 1961. English translation by Patrick Bowles and Samuel Beckett. Paris: Olympia Press, 1955. New York: Grove Press, 1955. Reprinted in *Three*. New York: Grove Press, 1965.

More Pricks than Kicks. London: Chatto & Windus, 1934. Reprint. London: Calder & Boyars, 1966. New York: Grove Press, 1972.

Murphy. English translation. London: Routledge, 1938. Reprint. New York: Grove Press, 1957. French translation. Paris: Bordas, 1947. Reprint. Paris: Editions de Minuit, 1965.

"One Evening" ("Un Soir"). French translation. In *Minuit* 37 (Jan. 1980): 2–3. English translation. In *Journal of Beckett Studies*, 6 (Autumn 1980):7–8.

"Ping" ("Bing"). French translation. Paris: Editions de Minuit, 1966. Reprinted in *Têtes-mortes*. Paris: Editions de Minuit, 1967. English translation. In *No's Knife: Collected Shorter Prose, 1945–1966*. London: Calder & Boyars, 1967.

"Sounds" and "Still 3." In *Essays in Criticism* 28, no. 2 (April 1978):155–57.

Stories and Textes for Nothing (*Nouvelles et Textes pour rien*). French translation. Paris: Editions de Minuit, 1955; 3d ed., 1965. English translation by Richard Seaver, Anthony Bonner, and Samuel Beckett. New York: Grove Press, 1967.

The Unnamable (*L'Innommable*). French translation. Paris: Editions de Minuit, 1953. Reprint. 1969. English translation. New York: Grove Press, 1958. Reprinted in *Three Novels*. New York: Grove Press, 1965.

Watt. English translation. Paris: Olympia Press, 1953. 3d ed. New York: Grove Press, 1959. French translation by Ludovic and Agnès Janvier and Samuel Beckett. Paris: Editions de Minuit, 1968.

Worstward Ho. London: John Calder, 1983.

Poetry

Collected Poems in English and French. London: John Calder, 1977.

Mirlitonnades (35 short poems in French, written 1976–78). Paris: Editions de Minuit, 1978.

Poemes. Paris: Editions de Minuit, 1968.

Poems in English. London: Calder & Boyars, 1961.

Secondary Works

Biography

Bair, Deirdre. *Samuel Beckett: A Biography*. New York and London: Harcourt Brace Jovanovich, 1978. Still the only biography available on Beckett to date, and though ambitious in scope, understandably incomplete.

Selected Critical Studies

Admussen, Richard. *The Samuel Beckett Manuscripts*. Boston: G. K. Hall, 1970. A close examination of unpublished manuscripts and early versions of published work.

Armstrong, Gordon S. *Samuel Beckett, W. B. Yeats, and Jack Yeats: Images and Words*. Lewisburg, Pa.: Bucknell University Press, 1990; London and Toronto: Associated University Presses, 1990. An informative examination of the literary influence of W. B. Yeats and the artistic influence of painter Jack Yeats on Beckett's work.

Ben-Zvi, Linda. *Samuel Beckett*. Boston: Twayne Publishers, 1986. A cogent study of Beckett's complete works whose comprehensive scope has necessitated a brief coverage of each text.

Bloom, Harold, ed. *Modern Critical Interpretations of Samuel Beckett's "Endgame."* New York: Chelsea House Publishers, 1988. A representative selection of eight of the best critical interpretations of *Endgame*, reprinted here in the chronological order of their original publication. It duplicates three essays by Adorno, Kenner, and Easthope previously anthologized by Bell Gale Chevigny.

Chevigny, Bell Gale, ed. *Twentieth Century Interpretations of "Endgame": A Collection of Critical Essays*. Englewood Cliffs, N.J.: Prentice Hall, 1969. A representative selection of eight significant essays on *Endgame* concerning character, theme, structure, and philosophical and literary comparisons.

Coe, Richard. *Samuel Beckett*. New York: Grove Press, 1964. An early study emphasizing Beckett's philosophical background.

Cohn, Ruby. *Back to Beckett*. Princeton, N.J.: Princeton University Press, 1973. A detailed study of Beckett's fiction and drama that also includes a scrupulous chronology of Beckett's work.

———. *Just Play*. Princeton, N.J.: Princeton University Press, 1980. Deals specifically with Beckett's plays and includes informative commentary on Beckett as stage director of his own work.

———. *Samuel Beckett: The Comic Gamut*. New Brunswick, N.J.: Rutgers University Press, 1962. A crucial study of the comic elements in

Bibliography

Beckett's fiction and drama, using Bergson's catalog of comic techniques.

Cooke, Virginia, comp. *Beckett on File*. London and New York: Methuen, 1985. A handy selection of comments by critics on Beckett's plays when first performed.

Esslin, Martin. *The Theatre of the Absurd*. Rev. ed. Garden City, N.Y.: Doubleday-Anchor, 1969. A seminal work, identifying the modern "absurdist" movement and placing Beckett in context with such writers as Adamov, Ionesco, and Genêt.

Fehsenfeld, Martha, and Dougald McMillan. *Beckett at Work*. London: John Calder, 1987. A collection of interviews with those involved in major productions of Beckett's plays.

Gontarski, S. E. *The Intent of Undoing in Samuel Beckett's Dramatic Texts*. Bloomington: Indiana University Press, 1985. Contains a detailed study of the sources, false starts, and preliminary versions of *Fin de partie* and of *Fin de partie* itself.

Gontarski, S. E., ed. *On Beckett: Essays and Criticism*. New York: Grove Press, 1986. A highly informative selection of essays representing the range of Beckett's fiction and drama, as well as the historical and ideological scope of the criticism that engages it.

Helsa, David H. *The Shape of Chaos: An Interpretation of the Art of Samuel Beckett*. Minneapolis: University of Minnesota Press, 1971. An examination of Beckett's fiction and drama to 1971 from the perspective of the history of ideas.

Henning, Sylvie Debevec. *Beckett's Critical Complicity: Carnival, Contestation, and Tradition*. Lexington: The University of Kentucky Press, 1988. A hermeneutic study of Beckett's fiction and drama.

Homan, Sidney. *Beckett's Theaters: Interpretations for Performance*. Lewisburg, Pa.: Bucknell University Press, 1984; London and Toronto: Associated University Presses, 1984. A detailed study of Beckett's dramatic works that have been performed in English, focusing on, among other things, the major themes and images, the role of the audience, and the visual and verbal dimensions of Beckett's drama.

Kalb, Jonathan. *Beckett in Performance*. Cambridge, New York, and Melbourne: Cambridge University Press, 1989. Offers critical documentation on some 70 or more major Beckett productions in Europe and America between 1978 and 1987, as well as interviews with pertinent actors and directors involved.

Kenner, Hugh. *Samuel Beckett: A Critical Study*. New York: Grove Press, 1961. Analyzes the formal elements, methods, situations, and philosophical and mathematical domains of Beckett's works.

Knowlson, James, and John Pilling. *Frescoes of the Skull: The Later Prose and Drama of Samuel Beckett*. New York: Grove Press, 1979. Collection of essays on Beckett's first attempts at prose and drama, his posttrilogy prose, and drama after *Endgame*.

Kott, Jan. *Shakespeare Our Contemporary*. Translated by Boleslaw Taborski. Garden City, N.Y.: Doubleday, 1964. Includes, among other things, a significant chapter entitled "*King Lear* or *Endgame*" (87–124), which contrasts the characters and situations in *Lear* with those of *Godot* and *Endgame*.

Lyons, Charles R. *Samuel Beckett*. Grove Press Modern Dramatists Series. New York: Grove Press, 1983. A detailed analysis of the theatrical images of character, space, and time in Beckett's most significant stage plays, radio dramas, television scripts, and film.

McMillan, Dougald, and Martha Fehsenfeld. *Beckett in the Theatre: The Author as Practical Playwright and Director*. Volume 1. London: John Calder, 1988; New York: Riverrun Press, 1988. A crucial study of the evolution of Beckett's stage plays from the original concept to more and more refined forms worked out in performance.

Pilling, John. *Samuel Beckett*. London and Boston: Routledge and Kegan Paul, 1976. A thorough account of Beckett's complete work up to 1976, based on his personal, intellectual, cultural, and literary background.

Reid, Alec. *All I Can Manage, More than I Could: An Approach to the Plays of Samuel Beckett*. Chester Springs, Pa.: Dufour Editions, 1968. Focuses specifically on Beckett's plays (from *Godot* to *Come and Go*) and the impact they can produce on theater audiences.

Robinson, Michael. *The Long Sonata of the Dead: A Study of Samuel Beckett*. New York: Grove Press, 1969. Contains a perceptive analysis of *Endgame* as a "terrifying insight into the loveless skull of the human world at the close of its career."

Schneider, Alan. *Entrances: An American Director's Journey*. New York: Viking Penguin, 1986. Autobiography of the American stage and television director "most favored" by Beckett, Albee, and Pinter, containing personal accounts of Schneider's directing of the American premieres of major Beckett dramatic works.

Webb, Eugene. *The Plays of Samuel Beckett*. Seattle: University of Washington Press, 1972. A chronological examination of Beckett's works for stage, radio, television, and cinema, focusing on the attitudes, problems, visions, and relationships of the characters and the imagery, underlying patterns, and approaches to the plays.

Wellwarth, George E. *The Theater of Protest and Paradox: Developments in the Avant-Garde Drama*. Rev. ed. New York: New York University Press, 1971. Contains a short but provocative commentary on Beckett's drama, entitled "Life in the Void" (41–56).

Index